Praise for Ike Vanden ~~Eykel~~ he has written or co-authored:

"When it comes to divorce Texas style, Mr. Vanden Eykel is the reigning king."

The Dallas Morning News

"As I read, I felt like I was listening to a trusted friend, who is also a highly experienced family lawyer."

Jane Klafter
Allen

"(*Protecting Your Assets From A Texas Divorce*) ... is intended to help individuals prepare financial information and records before their first consultation."

McKinney Messenger

"I actually read this cover to cover. What an interesting read."

KTBC Channel 7
Austin

"I recommend this book to any lawyer involved in the area of family law and I have placed it on the suggested reading list for all litigants in my court."

William W. Harris
Judge, 233rd Judicial District
Fort Worth

"(Vanden Eykel's) professional, yet compassionate approach to divorce in Texas makes this book a wonderful way to access sound legal advice at a fraction of an hourly attorney's fee."

Amazon.com

Lone Star Divorce

What Everyone Should Know
About Family Breakups in Texas

Ike Vanden Eykel | Sharla Fuller

Published by
PSG Books
9603 White Rock Trail, Suite 312 Dallas, Texas 75238
800 465-1508, 214 340-6223
upshaw@psgbooks.com

LONE STAR DIVORCE:
The NEW Edition

© 2008 by Ike Vanden Eykel, Sharla Fuller
and Professional Solutions Group

Library of Congress Cataloging-in-Publication Data

Vanden Eykel, Ike, 1949-
  Lone star divorce / by Ike Vanden Eykel, Sharla Fuller. -- New ed.
    p. cm.
  ISBN-13: 978-0-9749461-2-2
  ISBN-10: 0-9749461-2-5
  1.   Divorce suits--Texas--Popular works. 2.   Divorce--Law and
legislation--Texas--Popular works. I. Fuller, Sharla, 1967- II. Title.
  KFT1300.Z9V36 2007
  346.76401'66--dc22
                        2007041141

Notice

State laws, legal precedents, tax codes and regulations vary greatly from one jurisdiction to another and change over time. The reader should not use this book for specific legal advice. Every divorce case and post-divorce action is unique, requiring the advice of those versed in the laws of the jurisdiction where the action is taken.

It must be understood, therefore, that this book will provide readers with a general overview related to the divorce process and post-divorce issues, so they may take legal action or otherwise address these issues better informed.

Reading this book does not establish an attorney-client relationship between the reader and the authors. Consult an attorney for specific information related to your personal situation.

Ike Vanden Eykel / Sharla Fuller

Table of Contents

Part One   Where to Begin

The History of Custody
Types of Custody
Texas Law Favors Joint Custody
When Is Sole Custody Appropriate?
Who Should Be the Primary Custodian?
What You Should Know Before a Custody Fight
Custody/Visitation Problems
Standard Visitation and Access
Sharing Your Children
Parenting Classes

Calculating Child Support
Special Circumstances
Child Support Collection
Support for College

The Alimony Statute
The Alimony Reality
How the Court Decides
Temporary Spousal Support

Tax Liabilities and Refunds
Health Insurance for the Children
Health Insurance for the Spouse
Life Insurance

How Important is the House?
Consider Your Housing Options
Selling the House
Keeping the House Yourself
Transferring the Residence from One Spouse to the Other
Temporary Use by One Spouse

Impact of Keeping the Existing Mortgage
Tax Consequences

Part Four   Going to Court

Basic Rules for Giving Testimony

Part Five   Once Your Divorce Becomes Final

Introduction

There is plenty of good news about divorce in Texas. The number of divorces in the state is down rather dramatically. The conventional wisdom has been that half of all marriages end in divorce. That statistic is no longer correct. After divorce peaked at almost 65% of marriages in the early 1980s, the percentage of those breakups has waned to about 43% lately. This translates into almost 30,000 fewer divorces in 2005 than the annual total a generation before, even with significant population increases.

Of course, there are still 75,000 to 80,000 divorces a year in Texas, and that's nothing to celebrate. Neither is the fact that fewer people are getting married and that is the main reason divorce numbers are declining. Fewer marriages mean fewer divorces. For the first time in the history of our nation, more single adults than married ones are living alone or together without marriage, and this is a turnabout from the historical beginnings of our state.

Even before there was a state of Texas, there was divorce in this area of the Southwest. It all started with the Texas Divorce Act of 1841, enacted during the Republic of Texas. This Act preceded statehood by four years. Back then, Texas was a vast wilderness populated by very few people. There were few grounds for dissolving a marriage. No attorneys specialized in divorce and there were no courts that handled family cases exclusively.

In fact, there were so few divorces that family issues were considered trivial matters of law. When cases came to court, witnesses usually were not called and there were few, if any, experts in divorce and the welfare of children. The Texas Divorce Act, an amalgam of English common law and ancient Roman custom, had a simple way of approaching property. In most cases, the man was king unless he agreed to bestow property upon his soon-to-be ex. In a prime example of the evolution of social thought, children were considered the father's property and usually stayed with him.

Throughout the 19th and early 20th centuries, as Texas remained mostly rural, divorce was an option only in the most extreme circumstances — a spouse abandoning the family, becoming mentally incapacitated or engaging in the worst domestic violence.

During World War II, suddenly men were thousands of miles from home while their wives worked in the factories and took care of themselves and their children. At the end of the war, women welcomed their men home. They didn't, however, welcome the end of that freedom. The number of divorces began to grow through the late 1940s, 50s and 60s, and splitting up became easier and more accepted with the adoption of no-fault statutes in the 1970s.

The increase in personal freedom during the last few decades may have been good for individual well-being, but it has played havoc on the institution of marriage. We began to see divorce, inevitably, as a time for mean-spirited, nasty action. Divorce has meant that happy lives must necessarily end. Men complain that they lost their shirts in the divorce, while statistics show that many women and their children are condemned to poverty. To combat much of this guerilla action on the part of divorcing couples, the family law bar introduced mediation and collaborative law, which have made great positive differences in the conduct of divorce proceedings and their aftermath.

Many people believe the best answer to the problem is to make divorce more difficult to obtain. Some states are rethinking their no-fault statutes, so that married people must have a real and compelling reason for divorce. Some would make it more difficult for people to get married in the first place. But it's tough to socially engineer the results you want.

If people are going to continue to divorce, as they surely are, we hope this and other books on the subject foster an attitude of success during divorce to improve the lives of divorcing people and their children. The idea is that your family can emerge from divorce safe and sane. People can rebuild their lives. Children do not have to be scarred for life. A successful divorce is a process of getting to yes so that people can move on constructively. *LONE STAR DIVORCE: The NEW Edition* is meant to offer a breath of fresh air in the family courts, recognizing the evolution in this state over the past decade from open warfare to emphasis on the constructive life after divorce.

This book is based on the statutes and controlling case law in Texas at the time of publication. We take no responsibility for changes in the law between the publication date and the time you read this. But when changes in an aspect of divorce are anticipated, we try to make you aware of that possibility in this text.

We hope you make use of the extensive glossary of divorce terms we have compiled at the back of this book to enhance your understanding of divorce law and customs.

LONE STAR DIVORCE: The NEW Edition should not be used as a replacement for specific legal advice. It is not a how-to book. A successful divorce takes place when you work in tandem with a family law specialist, your friends and family to make it happen. Sometimes you have need of other professionals with expertise in such disciplines as financial planning, taxes, real estate or family therapy to help you through the process. At the back of this book, we have included a list of professionals who are not family lawyers but are experienced with divorce.

We would like to thank our clients, colleagues, families and friends for their help in this endeavor. We would also like to acknowledge the help of our editors at PSG Books, namely Alyssa Radcliff and Larry Upshaw.

This book contains the knowledge and experience of many people working together to make a Lone Star divorce one you can emerge from with your dignity intact.

Ike Vanden Eykel and Sharla Fuller

About the Authors

Ike Vanden Eykel is one of America's top divorce lawyers, author of the regional bestseller, *Successful Lone Star Divorce* (1998), and co-author of *Protecting Your Assets From A Texas Divorce* (2006). Managing partner of Koons, Fuller, Vanden Eykel & Robertson, the Southwest's largest family law firm, he is board certified in both family law and civil trial law. He came to prominence during the 1980s as a champion of fathers' rights, but *Vogue* magazine named him one of the Top Lawyers for Women in Texas. Ike was selected by *Town & Country* magazine as one of America's Top 10 Divorce Lawyers and has been featured in *Texas Monthly* as one of the Top 100 Attorneys in Texas.

In 2007, *The Dallas Morning News* dubbed him the "reigning king" of Texas divorce as well as the state's "most powerful divorce attorney" for his creative approaches to complex problems affecting divorcing people with large marital estates. Ike has very discreetly represented many rich and famous Texans. After handling an especially contentious divorce for a Park Cities housewife, he was depicted in the book *My Husband Is Trying To Kill Me* and a made-for-TV movie, *Dead Before Dawn*.

Besides writing books for the divorcing public, he co-authors an on-going series known as the *Texas Family Law Practice Guide* that is used by family law attorneys.

Active in the Dallas Bar Association, Ike is scheduled to become DBA president in 2010.

Sharla Fuller has been selected as one of the Top 50 Women Attorneys in Texas by her peers and has been listed as a Texas Super Lawyer featured in *Texas Monthly* magazine.

She began her legal career in East Texas before joining Koons, Fuller, Vanden Eykel & Robertson in 2000.

Sharla is board certified in family law. She is also a member of the Texas Academy of Family Law Specialists, the Family Law Section of the State Bar of Texas, the Family Law Section of the Dallas Bar Association, and the Texas Young Lawyers Association, and is admitted to practice before the U. S. District Courts for the Eastern and Northern Districts of Texas.

Sharla has authored and co-authored articles for family law seminars and has given speeches on family law topics.

LONE STAR DIVORCE: The NEW Edition is her first book for the general public.

Will This Marriage Never End?

When Alain and Cheryl Doucet filed for divorce, neither of them would have thought that six years would pass before they actually lived apart. They spent the first three fighting about the divorce. Cheryl wanted the house and custody of their two children and Alain didn't want to move out because that meant losing daily contact with his kids. After the three-year period, a judge ordered both parents to remain in the home until the youngest child turned 18 or graduated from high school.

Their sons described the next three years as "weird and divided." The couple lived like roommates with separate phone lines, televisions and refrigerator shelves. Each stayed away for long periods of time, trying to avoid the other, but conflicts were inevitable.

As the summer of their son's 18th birthday approached, Alain finally got tired of the arrangement and moved out to get remarried. Cheryl wasn't ready to let it go and tried to have him held in contempt of court. "I didn't care that he was getting married," she said, "but he was breaking a court order." The judge, who refused to comment about the case, did not prevent the breakup in the end.

From Associated Press reports

Part One:
Where to Begin

1

The Big Decision

DIVORCE, OR THE THREAT OF DIVORCE, begets a river of uncertainty. Whether you are happy, sad, confused or clinging to denial that you are confronting divorce, you're probably not in the best frame of mind for important decision making. Unfortunately, though, you have a lot of decisions to make, and some of them will affect the rest of your life and the lives of those around you — especially if you have children.

Imagine Life After Divorce

"Staying married can be one of life's great challenges," says Dr. Maryanne Watson, a board certified family psychologist in Dallas. "The tragedy of giving up on your relationship is that in many cases you'll repeat the same mistakes in your next relationship, only you'll have less money."

Divorce may seem like the answer to all your problems, but in many cases, you simply trade up to new difficulties. No matter how good your intentions, it is nearly impossible to escape the troubles created by divorce. Divorcing couples can become bitter and alienated. Their children often lose self-esteem and may be turned against one parent or the other. The ripple effect that divorce can have on children is seen in statistics indicating an increase in teenage crime, pregnancy, school problems and lifelong psychological difficulties. You must thoroughly consider how lives will be changed before you decide to divorce.

Step back and see yourself after the divorce for a moment. This thought can send you in a lot of different directions, but we won't sugarcoat this for you. Two important things will change the most — access to children and assets. For a time, you will probably have less money and property and perhaps a restricted schedule with your minor children.

Money Becomes Tighter

Most families can barely pay for one household. When you separate, you'll be running two households on the same amount of money. This creates a lot of financial pressure for both parties.

If you are the main breadwinner in the family before the divorce, you may have to give up a large portion of your income for months and years to come in child support or payments to help your spouse gain the skills to enter the work force. If you have not been working or have only worked part-time, chances are that you will now have to work full-time.

Property Gets Divided

Think about how you live now; the things you own and your current lifestyle. You may end up with greatly reduced retirement accounts, savings accounts, cars and household furnishings. Many couples buy bigger houses than they can easily afford, so when they break up there is no way for one of them to maintain the house. You must also factor in your debts. Credit cards, personal loans and other debts you've acquired as a married couple won't necessarily be split up according to who decided to spend the money.

Parenting is More Difficult

Being a single parent is hard. When the children are with you, you'll have to manage everything yourself. No matter how involved your spouse has been with the children, you no longer have someone to share all the daily responsibilities — making lunches, carpooling, hauling to piano lessons, dressing skinned knees and telling bedtime stories. You may not be able to go out with your friends as often, and if your child is sick, you'll be the sole caretaker. You may also experience some guilt when you see how much your children miss your spouse.

"Worst of all," says Dr. Watson, "nothing prepares you for being a part-time parent and having to miss out on part of your children's lives." One couple with two young children decided on joint custody. The father was a very involved parent, so they agreed to a 50/50 arrangement with the children spending alternate weeks in each household. After several months, the mother was miserable and told a friend, "I never intended to be a 50% mom when I had kids."

In addition to that, your children may eventually spend some of that time away from you with your ex's new partner, who will have a parenting role in your children's lives whether you like it or not. This can be a source of anger, resentment and frustration.

Now that you've taken a trip into your possible future, think about your present reality. As bad as it is, will living separately be any better, or is there some way to fix your broken relationship? When you move from marriage to divorce, your life turns upside down. Everything is different. You even shop for groceries with different priorities in mind. Some of these things can be a welcome change, but you may get more than you bargained for.

Consider Other Solutions

Dr. Watson says couples should consider how emotionally and financially devastating a divorce can be. Learning relationship skills is one of the best investments of time and money a couple can make. "It's often easier to learn those skills with the person you have a history with rather than starting over," she says.

One strategy Dr. Watson employs with couples who feel divorce is their only option is to have them live apart for three to six months. "Sometimes the couple simply has too much togetherness and needs to find a way to feel emotionally separate again." Although her clients may not like the rules — no speaking for the first two weeks, meeting only at her office, and no physical contact during the entire period — a trial separation provides a geographical boundary and a way to achieve emotional, physical and psychological separateness.

"In the beginning, the wife is often more invested in the relationship, and the husband looks forward to being on his own. The truth, though, is that men actually have a harder time being single. Until he comes to the conclusion that the relationship is worth the investment of time and energy needed to learn to do things differently, the wife has to be patient," says Dr. Watson. "With most couples, after a couple of months of separation and marital therapy, they become eager to be together again. At this point, many couples disobey the no-physical-contact rule, which I interpret as a hopeful sign of the viability of the relationship."

During one contentious divorce, the wife accused her husband of stealing household furnishings and financial documents. After hearing testimony on both sides, the judge ordered everyone to leave the courthouse to inspect the husband's residence. When they entered his home, they found the contested documents, along with confidential emails and letters regarding the case, strewn all over the floor. In addition, a thorough inspection of the home revealed the furniture, plants and paintings that the wife said he had stolen.

The judge then ordered everything taken to a storage unit, with the wife present to witness the return. As the deadline for returning the items neared, the wife's attorney attempted to call and email her several times without receiving a reply. He began to worry, as the wife had once suggested that her husband might harm her. Finally, the wife called back to confess that the coziness of the storage unit filled with furniture had inspired them to give their marriage another chance. So they began that second chance right there in the impromptu living room/storage facility.

Another way for couples to find emotional separateness is to learn to fight fairly. According to Dr. Watson, "When expressed correctly, anger is the best aphrodisiac there is. It sets a boundary."

Studies have shown that couples who fight fair stay married longer than couples who have a no-fight rule. "When you express anger," says Dr. Watson, "you are emotionally separate because you are expressing your honest thoughts and feelings, which are different from your partner's. When you do not fight because you fear hurting your partner's feelings, the two of you become too enmeshed emotionally. Fighting passionately, fairly and kindly keeps the relationship alive, vibrant and healthy."

Of course, it's not always possible to work it out. If you are in an abusive marriage or if your spouse spends every dollar in the house on alcohol or drugs, shopping or affairs, divorce may be your only option. You may not want a divorce, but your spouse insists on it. In these cases, you have little control over whether you get a divorce, but you can still have an impact on what kind of divorce you have.

A Successful Divorce

Ask yourself what kind of divorce you want. Many divorces separate the parties into victims and bullies. These divorces often escalate into screaming matches or quiet seething anger, and sometimes result in acts of revenge. Yet you have the power to choose a different kind of divorce — one where your kids are not burdened with unnecessary baggage — where you and your soon-to-be ex act like adults, instead of adolescents. It is possible for everyone to emerge emotionally and financially intact if you choose to make it happen.

Successful Divorce Principles

If a successful divorce is your goal, keep the following principles in mind:

- Look for resolution, not revenge.
- Don't confuse what's best for the children with what will gain you vengeance.
- Hire the most experienced family law attorney you can afford who matches your personality.
- Try to keep your divorce uncontested.
- Mediate or collaborate in good faith.
- Stockpile useful family information.
- Be truthful with your attorney.
- Work with your spouse to decide on a division of assets. If at all possible, don't let a judge or jury decide for you.
- Decide what's in the best interest of your children and follow that path.
- Be compassionate and generous when you can.
- If your spouse concedes something he or she doesn't have to, be grateful.
- If mediation fails, get ready for trial.
- Present yourself well before the judge or jury.
- Remember that if you don't get everything you want, your life is not over.
- Ask yourself: Will this divorce settlement leave me and my family in a good situation, whether I remarry or not?

In Texas during 2004, an average of 223 divorces and 489 marriages took place each day.[1] When you are in the midst of a divorce, getting married again may be the last thing on your mind, but life goes on and many people do remarry. Do not leave yourself financially wounded or in a difficult custody arrangement that will hinder your future happiness.

One young man gave his wife custody of their children and all the marital assets. On top of that, he agreed to exorbitant child support payments. The divorce was not his idea, but he gave in to all of his wife's demands, "because I didn't want my kids to suffer."

When asked about his attorney's role in negotiating the settlement, the man said, "I wanted to give my ex-wife all of that. I didn't think I needed an attorney." Three months after the divorce was settled, she moved 2,000 miles away to live with a man they had both considered a friend. The ex-husband was left with no money and significant debt, and he now sees his children and most of his assets once a year. Though still young, he feels unable to handle the emotional and financial obligations involved in starting a new relationship.

The best way to avoid such a tragedy is to consult with an expert in family law. You might think we suggest that simply because this is our profession. But in truth there is no limit to the foolishness we've seen divorcing people engage in before they hire an attorney. Do not sign any documents without the advice and approval of an attorney hired to represent you and only you. Sharing an attorney, either to save money or because you think you and your spouse can work out an agreement yourselves, is rarely a good idea. Under Texas law, an attorney can only represent one of you, which leaves the other side unprotected. If you use only one attorney, make sure he or she represents you and not your spouse.

Basic Truths of a Texas Divorce

Until recently, the divorce rate in Texas was higher than the national average. "Studies have shown that this was primarily because the average age at marriage has been younger here than in many other parts of the country," says Dr. Norval Glenn, professor of sociology at the University of Texas at Austin. "Also the divorce rate tends to be higher in parts of the country that experience rapid growth, where lots of people move in and there is high turnover in the population. This kind of atmosphere makes communities less cohesive and separates people from their extended families. It has been shown that close relationships with extended families tend to inhibit divorce."

In 2004, statistics showed the national divorce rate to be 3.7 divorces per 1,000 people.[2] In that same year, Texas finally dipped below the national average with 3.6 divorces per 1,000 people.[3] "The main factor in the changes we're seeing is that people are getting married later in life now. We know that marriages of young people are very likely to end in divorce, so the increase in the average age of marriage has reduced the divorce rate," says Dr. Glenn.

Each state sets its own divorce laws. While there are similarities from one state to another, there are also differences. Here are a few simple truths you should know about the divorce laws in Texas.

Truth #1:   Either person can ask for and receive a jury trial (although jury decisions that are binding on the court are limited).

Truth #2:   There is a 60-day waiting period from the date you file the divorce until it can be final, even if it is uncontested.

Truth #3:   If you and your spouse cannot agree on a division of property, a judge will divide it for you in a manner deemed to be "just and right." The judge may look at future earning capacity, who is at fault in the divorce and other criteria when deciding who gets what.

Truth #4:   Alimony is rare in Texas, unless you have no significant assets or means to support yourself, or unless you and your spouse agree to it.

Truth #5: The spouse who does not have primary custody of the children will, in almost every case, pay child support to the one who does. The amount of support is based on guidelines in the Texas Family Code.

Truth #6: Joint custody is preferred in Texas, which means you will likely share parental rights and duties with your ex. The amount of time you spend with the children, though, will not necessarily be equal.

Truth #7: Both you and your spouse will have significant access to your children after the divorce unless you agree otherwise or can show that such access would be harmful to the children.

Truth #8: Once a divorce is filed in Texas, you cannot stop it from happening if one of you wants to go through with it.

2

Once Your Mind is Made Up

SOMETIMES THE ONLY WAY to address the pain and confusion of a difficult marriage is to make the decision to divorce. It can be scary and liberating at the same time. Even though money may be tight for awhile and taking care of the children can be more difficult, by making the decision you're taking your fate into your own hands, and that can be empowering.

Genna always thought a big decision like getting a divorce would come to her like a bolt out of the blue, but instead the decision was a long, painful one. In college, Steve was charming and had a smile she couldn't resist. She saw how he looked at other women and knew he wandered now and then, but she thought that time and the responsibilities of a family would cure him. After the birth of their second child and Steve's big promotion at work, she began to feel the distance between them grow even wider.

There were signs that he still hadn't settled down, but she ignored them because she had a family to protect. His cellphone bills had hundreds of calls to one unfamiliar number, and charges he made on their credit cards puzzled her. The last straw was the bouquet of roses she received on Valentine's Day. Her husband had signed the card, but the message was intended for someone else. The florist had mixed up the two orders he placed. The next morning, Genna made an appointment with a lawyer to file for divorce.

Which Route to Take

Most divorces are resolved by one of four methods: direct negotiation, collaborative law, mediation or litigation. Below you will find a brief explanation of each one, so that you can begin to familiarize yourself with your options. Each of these methods is discussed in greater detail in later chapters.

Direct Negotiation

People usually use this method when they cannot afford any of the other options. In this approach, you and your spouse formulate a plan and have your lawyers do the paperwork, or you negotiate through letters and phone calls between your lawyers.

Collaborative Law

This is a relatively new kinder, gentler approach to handling a divorce and. During a series of sessions, you and your spouse sit down at a table with your attorneys. The four of you discuss all facets of the divorce and make agreements as you go along. Attorneys who practice collaborative law are usually trained in this method on providing legal advice, keeping the sessions on track and ensuring that you and your spouse treat each other fairly. Sessions end for the day if emotions get out of control.

Collaborative law is often less expensive, more private, more flexible and faster than litigation. The benefits depend upon the abilities of you and your spouse to compromise and adhere to the rules of the process. Couples who go through the collaborative process often report that they receive a fair settlement and emerge emotionally intact.

If you are leaning toward an alternative such as collaborative law, read Chapter 6 (starting on page 70) for a more complete explanation of the process.

Mediation

In Texas, a judge often orders mediation prior to a final trial. In mediation, you and your spouse try to forge an agreement on the division of assets, custody of your children and any other decisions that need to be made during the divorce. Typically, you and your attorney sit in one room while your spouse and his or her attorney sit in another. A mediator goes back and forth between the two rooms trying to help you reach an agreement. One side will make an offer which the mediator brings to the other side. You then accept the offer or make a counter-offer. The process goes like this until you decide everything or reach an impasse. Unlike a collaborative law divorce, which is handled in multiple meetings, mediation is usually accomplished in one exhausting day-long marathon session.

Once you reach all possible agreements, the attorneys present the agreements to the judge, who normally approves them. If you cannot reach an agreement on certain things or if you cannot agree on anything, then a trial date is set and the remaining issues are resolved through litigation.

Litigation

This is the most adversarial method of resolving a divorce. It is also the most public and expensive. It's handled in traditional courtroom style, where the attorneys try your case in front of a judge or jury. Tempers may flare and accusations fly as each attorney tries to find a smoking gun in the behavior of the opposing spouse.

This approach can be drawn out due to the nature of court. It can be damaging to both sides, including those who may be brought in to testify. If you and your spouse simply cannot agree, though, it may be the only way to dissolve the marriage. Keep in mind that the cost of a trial can leave you with fewer assets.

Financial Steps to Prepare for Divorce

Once you've decided to divorce, there are some things you should do right away to protect yourself financially.

1. Make a list of all of your assets and debts, whether you hold them separately or together. Make a copy of the latest statement for each loan and bank account or other investment account. Make copies of any other documents you have that show the value of physical assets that may be divided.

2. Request a copy of your credit report. Check this against your listing of debts.

3. If you do not have a credit history separate from your spouse, start building one. Begin by applying for a credit card or two. This is not a license to spend money but a way to start building credit in your own name. Without a personal credit history, you cannot qualify for a car loan, personal loan or mortgage on your own. You may also need to use a credit card to hire an attorney for the divorce.

4. Start saving money in a separate bank account that is in your name only. You may need this money to pay bills during the divorce. You will have to disclose these funds, but at least you will have immediate access to them.

5. Prepare yourself for a reduction in lifestyle. Divorce can be financially difficult for both partners in the short run.

6. Decide which assets you would like to keep and which you are willing to give up.

7. Learn the divorce laws. Texas is a community property state. The court must decide what constitutes community property and divide those assets. Depending on your case, the court may or may not divide the assets equally.

8. Gather the documents and other evidence necessary to prove any separate property claims.

Your Spouse's Evil Twin

You may think you know your spouse very well. But when it comes to divorce, people often act in ways that surprise you. Friends, family and even experts can encourage your spouse to act out of character. More than one person has described the experience this way: it's as though a relatively reasonable person walked out the door as soon as the divorce papers were filed and in walked an evil twin, ready to make a mess of the divorce.

Even if your ex is not acting differently, you may perceive it that way. "To make parting with someone easier, you often start focusing on their negative aspects," says Dr. Richard Warshak, a clinical psychologist and author of *Divorce Poison: Protecting the Parent-Child Bond from a Vindictive Ex.* "It's easy to rewrite history and remember only the bad things, but it's important to maintain a balanced view of your ex during this time." Focusing on the bad things will only make it harder to agree on a settlement and is not in the best interests of you or your children.

If you find that your ex acts negatively toward you or attempts to use your children as pawns against you, your initial reaction may be to respond with the same behavior in return. This only increases the problem, but you may not know how else to deal with the situation. "If you continually say good things about your ex to your children and others," says Dr. Warshak, "it is much harder for your ex to act negatively toward you."

Restrict Your Story to a Limited Number of People

There is a critical point at the beginning of most divorces when one of you talks to too many people. Talking is very therapeutic and can help you get through this difficult time. But the other side in the divorce can distort your comments and those words may come back to haunt you. Plenty of divorces begin amicably, and then people start talking to others. Friends and family members often are brought into court to testify, especially when the custody of children is involved.

Be very selective about the people you choose to tell your deepest secrets. Every marriage has its ups and downs, and none of us are angels, but this is a time when all your dirty laundry is available for inspection if you allow it. Whether fact or fiction, everyone you know will have an opinion, such as, "I never liked him anyway," or "I always told you she was no good." People can say awful things to you and about you, and when you've finally had enough, the lid blows and a divorce that you might have settled calmly becomes a desperate struggle.

To keep this from happening, sit down and make a list of friends and family who must be told or who will find out through the grapevine. Decide how much you want to tell people and how much you want them to tell you.

At this early stage, many couples reconcile. When we're mad or upset, we rarely tell others about the good things, and it's embarrassing to have to take back every bad thing you said about your spouse if you decide not to go through with the divorce. You'll probably have to listen to frustrated friends and family who cannot believe you plan to stay with your spouse after hearing what you've endured. When in doubt, keep the most damaging details to yourself for the time being.

Family members and friends should rally to your defense at a time like this, but there is no guarantee that they will. Be prepared for skeptical looks and probing questions like, "Why on earth would you get divorced? You'll never marry that well again."

The people asking these questions probably don't know all the secrets of your marriage, like the fact that he had numerous affairs or that she racked up tens of thousands of dollars in credit card debt. Family and friends may agree with your actions, but be prepared for the opposite reaction. If the blessing of those close to you is important, be prepared to lay out the facts of the case in excruciating detail.

Q&A

*Can I date while the divorce
is ongoing?*

"You should never date during the divorce. It makes a bad appearance and might cause additional issues that drag out the divorce and drive up the cost. If you have children, it is not good for them to see you with a partner who isn't their parent at that critical time. Some people will date anyway. Be aware that your emails and phone calls might be entered into evidence, or an investigator might follow you. And under no circumstances should you introduce your children to your new friend."

*Jeff Domen
Family Law Attorney*

Telling Your Children

Telling your children about the divorce can be one of the most difficult steps. Chances are the kids already know the problem exists, but everyone will be better able to adjust once it's out in the open. It's important that they hear it from you or your spouse, preferably together if you can manage it in a civil manner, before they hear it from someone else.

Keep in mind that children often blame the person who breaks the news to them. Telling the children as a couple usually is the best approach, since you will both be there to reassure the kids and answer questions. Talk with your spouse about what you will say. It often helps to remind the children that you love them and even though you will no longer be living together as husband and wife, you will not stop being their mother and father.

The idea of staying together for the children has long been debated. There is evidence that the age of your children at the time of your divorce is a factor that may help in making your decision. "Studies have consistently shown that divorce may not have much of a psychological effect on children under the age of two," says UT sociology professor Dr. Norval Glenn. "For older children, those approaching adulthood, the short term effects can be severe but the developmental effects are not significant in the long term."

When you talk to your children alone, resist the urge to lay blame on your spouse. Children are the product of both of you and should not be involved in your adult problems and battles.

One woman's husband stayed drunk and away from home for weeks at a time. He refused to work while she brought in all the income and took care of their three kids. The last straw was when she found out that he raided their daughter's college fund to pay for his girlfriend's breast enlargement. If anyone deserved to badmouth someone, she certainly did, but she resisted the temptation to destroy him in the eyes of his children. Instead, she extracted a promise that if she would keep quiet, he would return the money and agree to certain other demands. He agreed and together they told the kids about the pending divorce. It wasn't easy, but it was the right thing to do.

Helping Your Children Through the Divorce

Regardless of the feelings you and your spouse have for each other, your children need to know that you will both continue to love and care for them and that they did not cause the divorce. According to Dr. Ray Levy, child psychologist and author of *Try and Make Me!*, a book for parents and teachers dealing with difficult children, you must continue to maintain a positive parental relationship with your kids. You have a responsibility to protect them from any feelings you might have of failure, disappointment and resentment and help them transition to a life after divorce.

When you talk to your children about the divorce and how their lives will change, Dr. Levy recommends using the following statements as the foundation for your conversations:

- We both love you very much and that will continue.
- You were conceived in love, and that won't change.
- Our divorce is not your fault.
- We will always help and protect you.
- We cannot get back together as husband and wife. Do not hope for it.
- We are divorcing as husband and wife, not as mother and
- father.
- We will communicate and work together on matters concerning you.
- We will not say bad things about each other.
- You will not have to choose between us.
- We will support each other's rules.
- We want you to do well in school and life.

- We do not expect you to have problems because we are divorcing and we do not expect you to use our divorce as an excuse for bad behavior.
- We do not know all the details about the future, but we will tell you as soon as we know.
- You will be able to visit all your grandparents, aunts and uncles, and they will not say bad things about either of us.
- You have our permission to mind, respect, and love your other parent, stepparent or significant other.

If you find that no matter how hard you try, you cannot keep your feelings from interfering with your ability to parent, you may need to get outside help. A counselor can teach you how to set aside your negative emotions when you interact with your children, so that you can help them transition to a positive post-divorce life.

3

Hiring a Family Lawyer

WHEN MARIE AND TONY DECIDED to get divorced, they agreed to keep it simple, inexpensive and civil. They sat down together, divided their property and agreed that their daughter would live with Marie. Then Tony submitted their decisions to the attorney who handled things for his trucking company and asked him to draw up the papers.

Marie moved into an apartment, and since things were going smoothly between them, she agreed that their daughter would stay at Tony's until the end of the school semester.

When the papers were ready, Tony brought them to Marie to be signed. "There's only one problem," he told her. "You know I don't want custody. But you haven't been in your apartment long enough, so the attorney says the judge will want the papers to say that I get custody. It's just a formality."

Marie didn't have her own counsel. Tony assured her that his lawyer was acting as counsel for both of them. She signed the divorce agreement, genuinely believing that she would still get custody of their child because Tony said she would.

Q&A

*Can one attorney represent
both of us?*

"One attorney cannot represent the interests of two clients in the same divorce. Unfortunately, I see it happen over and over again where the more streetwise spouse tries to convince the other that one attorney can represent both sides. If you do not hire the attorney to represent you exclusively, under Texas law that attorney has absolutely no obligation to look out for your interests. This could be devastating to your future, both financially and for your children."

*Liz Porter
Family Law Attorney*

Within a few days, Tony's mood toward her changed. When she called to talk to her daughter, she learned that his female assistant had moved into the house. When Marie asked Tony when her daughter was coming to live with her, he informed her, "The papers say I get custody," and hung up the phone.

Trust Cautiously

Many problems in divorce are caused by misplaced trust. The best pathway to a successful divorce seems to require you to walk a fine line between being genial and assertive. Just because you've known your spouse for years does not mean you can accurately predict his or her behavior in a divorce. It is important to stand up for yourself and make sure that someone is looking out for your interests and the interests of your children.

In the case of Marie and Tony, things were eventually straightened out. Marie got custody of her daughter, but it took a tremendous financial and emotional toll to go back to court to prove that he deceived her and that he had obtained the original divorce agreement through fraud. Marie learned a hard lesson—that she could no longer trust someone who had been such a big part of her life.

Representing Yourself

In Texas, you have the right to represent yourself in court. You become a pro se or self-represented litigant, an increasing practice across the country. The decision to represent yourself should not be made lightly. Consider the complexity of your case, the amount of time needed to inform yourself about the process and your emotional state at this time of your life.

People have many reasons for wanting to represent themselves. You may feel you can't afford an attorney, have a severe dislike for attorneys or feel you have a simple case and do not need one. You may have watched enough court shows on television that you think you can do it on your own. Whatever the reason, do some research and at least interview a couple of attorneys before making this decision.

Representing yourself can be tricky, since you probably don't know the rules of court. A judge may hold you to the same standards expected of any lawyer. You will need to know how to prepare the forms correctly, how to address the judge properly and how to present evidence in your case. For instance, if you have separate assets, it is important to know how to prove they aren't part of the community estate or they could be divided and at least half of them awarded to your spouse.

Family court Judge Marilea Lewis says that when children are involved, it's always better to have an attorney represent you. There is often critical information in these cases that you may not know how to get admitted into evidence. One of the most common objections in these cases is hearsay, and most hearsay objections are sustained. The hearsay rule basically prohibits secondhand testimony at a trial. For example, if a child told an aunt something one of the parents did, the aunt usually is not allowed to testify about it if the opposing party objects under the hearsay rule.

"Even when two litigants represent themselves," Judge Lewis says, "if they know about the hearsay rule, they can often object and get much of the other party's evidence left out of the trial."

A lack of knowledge slows down the legal system and takes up more of the court's time, so some urban counties in Texas are attempting to help pro se litigants learn the process. There are also forums and clinics hosted by men's and women's rights groups that can teach you about the process. If you plan to represent yourself, properly educate yourself beforehand.

If your case is truly uncontested, does not involve children and has little property to divide, representing yourself can be a viable alternative. If you do have children, a substantial amount of property, or other complex arrangements between you and your spouse, representing yourself is rarely a wise decision. You need the advice of a family law expert if you want to successfully negotiate a fair settlement and document it properly.

Match Your Attorney to Your Circumstances

Don't hire the first attorney you come across in the Yellow Pages. Be a smart consumer and take the time to find one who meets your needs at a price you can afford. Depending on your situation, you may want an attorney with experience in a particular aspect of divorce. Some specialize in finding hidden assets. Others have a knack for fending off trouble from the opposition or obtaining custody of children.

Whatever your need and your budget, there is an attorney out there who is right for you. Of the more than 1,100,000 attorneys practicing in the United States, approximately 70,000 are licensed right here in Texas.[4] Of those, roughly 4,400 handle some family law cases.[5]

One of the best ways to locate an attorney is to ask people to recommend someone. If you have friends or relatives in your area who have gotten a divorce, ask who they used and if they were happy with the results. If you know an attorney who practices in another field of law, ask him or her for a referral to a family lawyer. Your local bar association may have a referral service that categorizes attorneys by specialty. You can also ask marriage counselors, accountants, financial planners, business managers and clergy. Because of their professions, they often know family lawyers with good reputations and track records.

Interviewing Lawyers

Once you have the names of several family lawyers, call and schedule initial interviews with each of them. You should interview at least two, but don't forget to ask if the attorney charges a fee up front for this first interview. Some do and some don't.

Q&A

*How much is the divorce
going to cost?*

"This is a logical question to ask at the beginning, and once I know the facts of the case, I can give an intelligent estimate. I don't know what I'm facing until I open the box that contains everything about a couple's married life."

Ike Vanden Eykel

In the initial interview, an attorney will want to go over the basic history of your marriage and the issues involved in the divorce. Be as straightforward as possible and tell the attorney your good points as well as your bad ones. Lawyers are under an ethical obligation not to disclose the information you tell them, unless you consent to the disclosure. Do not worry about the shock value of what you disclose. Experienced family lawyers have heard it all. Adultery, physical abuse, gambling, substance abuse and unusual sexual practices are things they hear about on a regular basis.

In this first visit, a lawyer will try to determine the basic issues in the case and summarize the major assets and liabilities at stake. You can speed this up by bringing a detailed list of debts and assets with you, along with a written history of your marriage and the reasons for the divorce.

Information to have at the first meeting includes:

- Number of years or months you've been married
- Names and ages of your children and any special needs they may have
- Reasons for the divorce
- Your perception of the fault of either spouse (i.e., adultery, excessive gambling)
- Description of your parental relationships with the children and how you share childcare responsibilities
- Work history for each of you
- Income for each of you
- Summary of your community assets and debts

At the interview stage, ask questions about the attorney's experience. Ask for a description of the family law cases he or she has handled and the results. If you have any particular needs, such as keeping a family business intact, you'll want to know the attorney's experience handling this type of case and the resources (i.e. expert witnesses) available to provide assistance. Don't allow an attorney to generalize about past accomplishments. Request specific information about the attorney's experience with trials, including jury trials, mediation and collaborative law cases. If you doubt the attorney's capabilities, move down your list.

Determine if your personality is compatible with that of a particular attorney. By the time the divorce is final, this attorney will know your life story, including the good, the bad and the ugly. You'll also talk on a regular basis, so choose someone you won't mind spending a great deal of time with while the divorce is ongoing.

If you are angry about the divorce, you may want to hire the meanest junkyard dog in existence, but meanness only breeds more anger, and anger usually results in roadblocks. What you need instead is an attorney who can channel that meanness in a way that helps you. Maybe the better option is to find an attorney who can successfully settle your case quickly and quietly.

At the end of the initial meeting, both you and the attorney will decide whether to proceed together. If the answer is yes, the lawyer will probably give you some homework — a list of additional information to gather. Also, you will be asked to sign and return an agreement covering legal fees and expenses.

How Much Do Attorneys Charge?

The more experienced and specialized the attorney, the more he or she will charge. Deciding how high up the lawyer ladder to go is usually a matter of economics coupled with the facts of the case. If you have little property to divide and no children, a less experienced attorney will do fine. If you own a large home, several cars, some investments, a retirement account or two, or a small business, you may be surprised at your net worth, and you'll want to hire someone with the experience to protect it.

- Young attorneys who handle many different kinds of cases, such as family law, criminal and real estate might ask for a retainer of $1,500. From that they will subtract their time at $100 to $200 per hour.

- More experienced attorneys who spend most of their time on divorce work will expect a retainer of $2,500 to $15,000 and charge $200 to $400 per hour. Most attorneys at this level are board certified in family law by the Texas Board of Legal Specialization, an arm of the State Bar of Texas.
- A handful of Texas attorneys who are considered the best in the nation at their specialty charge a retainer of $25,000 or more and bill for their time at an hourly rate of $500 to $750.

Keeping Fees Reasonable

Like many professionals, lawyers get paid by the hour. When you hire a mechanic to fix your car or a plumber to fix your leaky pipes, you get an estimate first. Due to the nature of divorce, though, it's nearly impossible for an attorney to give you more than a ballpark estimate at the start.

Attorneys bill not just for their own time, but also for the time spent by other attorneys and staff members who work on your case. It's important to know when the clock is ticking so that your bills are not unnecessarily high. Every minute you meet with your attorney or talk on the phone is billable time. This may seem obvious, but it can be hard to remember while you're sitting in your attorney's office enjoying a cup of coffee and chatting about your case. It's only natural for you to talk about this tumultuous event in your life with someone you trust, but keep in mind that the more time you spend recounting your exierences, the more money it will cost you. Your attorney may become a friend, but he or she is still a professional on the clock.

Each time you are about to talk to your attorney, sit down beforehand and write out your questions and any information you need to convey during the conversation. Then stick to the list.

Ten Strategies for Controlling Legal Fees

You will need to spend money on your case to ensure that you receive good legal advice and get as fair a settlement as possible, but there are things you can do to control fees.

1. Tell your attorney that money is an issue for you.
2. Be aware that any time your attorney or a member of the law firm's staff works on your case, talks to you on the phone or meets with you, it costs you money.
3. Do not use your attorney or the staff as a counseling service.
4. Help your attorney by collecting financial information, tracking down documents and handling other chores so that someone else is not hired to do this.
5. Each time you do something designed to keep your fees down, tell your attorney you expect it to lower your bill. A friendly reminder never hurts.
6. Learn to distinguish a real emergency from the panic of divorce. Emergency calls to your attorney after hours and on weekends can cost you a lot of money.
7. Let your attorney know which assets are important to you and which ones are not. Fighting on too many fronts can be expensive and difficult.
8. Don't encourage (or allow) your attorney to spend time fighting for an asset that is worth less than the cost of acquiring it.
9. If you and your spouse can settle issues on your own, such as the custody of your children or who should run the family business, do so but get your attorney's advice before and after each meeting.
10. Never tell your attorney to do whatever it takes. This is the same as saying, "I don't care how much it costs."

Many things can be handled briefly over the phone. Face-to-face meetings usually take more time. Due to court schedules, family law experts often return phone calls late at night or from their homes. Keep in mind that this is family time and can be expensive.

Major developments in your case, either good or bad, can happen at night or over a weekend. Your instinct may be to pick up the phone and call your attorney, but respect his or her time — and your wallet — and make these calls only when it's truly necessary. Ask your attorney to define what is considered an emergency and when you should call.

Unfortunately, one of the biggest variables in the number of hours spent on a divorce is something you control the least — the behavior of your spouse. Most attorneys try to determine up front how much resistance to expect from the other side. If your spouse is combative and wants his or her day in court, you could be in for a lengthy and expensive battle.

A Word About Retainers

A retainer is essentially a down payment toward future legal fees, and most family lawyers require one. Asking for payment up front ensures that the lawyer will be paid for time spent and expenses incurred. Retainers ranging from $2,500 to $15,000 are common throughout Texas. Cases involving large estates, complicated financial issues or difficult child custody disputes may require a retainer of $25,000 or more.

As hours are billed on your case, the money is deducted from the retainer. As the balance drops below a certain point, you are asked to replenish the retainer. If your case goes to trial, you may have to replenish your retainer several times, as a contested trial can take several days of trial time and weeks of preparation. In the past, retainers were not considered refundable, even if the case settled quickly or the client became unhappy and hired another lawyer. In the case of a quick settlement, some high-powered attorneys justified this by saying that the other side was frightened away by their reputation alone and therefore hiring their firm was worth it. Today, people are wiser consumers of legal services and most attorneys refund any remaining balance of your retainer. The fee agreement you sign should be clear on this point.

You may feel hesitant about paying such a large sum of money up front, but retainers are often necessary to protect attorneys. Divorces can be highly emotional and most couples fight over money. It is only practical for your attorney to be assured of getting paid. You probably don't get paid for the work you do up front, but if the company you worked for was in turmoil, wouldn't you be nervous about waiting weeks or months for your check?

Attorneys know that if a client is unwilling to pay in the midst of a crisis, it's unlikely he or she will pay once the problem is solved. This is especially true if the matter isn't solved to the client's complete satisfaction. Attorneys are most productive working on their cases, not being debt collectors.

If money is tight or you lack access to funds until your divorce is settled, talk to your attorney. An effective attorney will find a way to secure sufficient funding.

You Will Probably Pay Your Own Fees

In times past, many attorneys took cases in which the husband was ordered to pay his wife's attorney fees at the end of a divorce. This practice is less common as the court system becomes more gender neutral, so few attorneys will depend on future payments from the other side.

Most attorneys want some money up front, but your attorney may be flexible if you actually have assets that may not be available at this time. If the assets are liquid enough that the attorney can expect to be paid at settlement or at the end of a trial, he or she will often work with you to get the divorce finalized.

Request Regular Bills

Your attorney should provide you with regular billing statements at least once a month, showing the time invested in your case, the expenses incurred and the unused balance of any retainer. If you do not receive regular bills, request them. You don't want to be surprised at the amount of money you owe when the case ends. There's nothing worse than spending tens of thousands of dollars in legal fees only to end up with assets worth much less.

If you or your spouse become difficult, your attorney will need to invest more hours in the case and fees will rise accordingly. Seeing how much a bad attitude costs may encourage you to compromise and get things settled.

Some people tell their lawyers to do whatever it takes. Giving your attorney this much freedom to spend your money rarely results in anything other than exorbitant legal bills. Monthly statements that detail services rendered can protect against out-of-control legal fees.

Talk About Expenses

Most attorneys itemize outside expenses, such as court filing fees, deposition transcripts and expert witnesses. Ask your attorney for a rundown of all anticipated costs. A good attorney will have no trouble explaining them to you.

Typical expenses incurred in a divorce proceeding include:

- Filing fees for a divorce action in Texas average around $200.
- Depositions of the opposing party and important witnesses are conducted prior to a trial. Costs are based on the length of the deposition. A court reporter usually records the testimony and can cost several hundred to many thousands of dollars.

- Pleadings, subpoenas and other related documents must be served on the opposing party. If time is of the essence, a special process server can deliver documents immediately, instead of waiting for the local sheriff's department to do it, which can sometimes take several weeks. A process server generally costs $50 to $100 or more per delivery, depending on how difficult it is to locate and serve the individual.
- Copies, faxes, expensive mailings and other costs associated with the case are often charged separately.
- Expert witnesses are necessary in many complex cases. Accountants, business consultants, real estate appraisers and psychologists are just a few of the experts who may be needed. Fees for their services vary by profession and the amount of time they are needed.

Form a Partnership with Your Attorney

The two of you should work together as a team, with information flowing in both directions. If there are any communication problems between you, address them immediately.

Your attorney should keep you informed of developments in your case, upcoming actions such as serving your spouse with divorce papers and any communications from your spouse's attorney. He or she should advise you in every instance.

Your attorney should also be specific about procedures, deadlines and costs involved in the process. Never tolerate an attorney's unwillingness to answer your questions or keep you in the loop. Your attorney works for you, and the two of you must work together.

Complete any homework assignments your attorney gives you as soon as possible. A good attorney will want to know all the relevant information about your marriage, the reasons for divorce and the overall history of your relationship. A written narrative from you can be extremely helpful in preparing your case. Make it as informative as possible without being too lengthy or negative. Prepare this information somewhere safe, such as at a trusted friend's house, and keep it in a place where your spouse cannot find it.

In addition, your lawyer will need a listing of assets and debts with as much detail as you can provide. If custody is an issue, you will need to supply extensive information about your children and the parenting history of you and your spouse. You should also provide a timeline of events, along with a witness list. This not only gives your attorney the information needed to formulate your case, but it makes you think about the events that have had a major impact on your marriage.

4

Nontraditional Living Arrangements

AS WE MENTIONED IN THE INTRODUCTION, a smaller proportion of the population is getting married each year. More Texans are opting for nontraditional living arrangements. Situations that do not fit within the typical mold of marriage and divorce may be handled by the legal system in ways that are different from the norm. This chapter attempts to cover the basics of common law marriage, people who separate after living together, children of unmarried parents, palimony and annulment.

Common Law Marriage

Texas is currently one of the nine states, along with the District of Columbia, that recognize common law marriage, though there are five other states that recognize common law marriages created prior to certain dates. Such a marriage in Texas lacks a marriage license and often a ceremony, but in all other aspects is the same under the law as a conventional marriage. The Texas Family Code says that in order to have a recognized common law marriage, a couple must:

- Agree that they are married (even though no formal ceremony may have taken place)
- Live together as husband and wife
- Represent to others that they are married

Essentially this means that you agreed to be married, even though you never took the formal steps of getting a license and having a wedding ceremony. You told friends and neighbors you were married and acted as husband and wife. You can sign a declaration at the county clerk's office attesting to the fact that you have entered into a common law marriage, but this begs the question: if you are in the county courthouse, why not just get married conventionally? A common law marriage is valid whether or not it is registered. The registration is merely a useful tool for determining whether the parties were actually married if they later disagree.

In the context of a divorce proceeding, you must first prove a common law marriage existed if you wish to use the laws and rules of divorce in dissolving your relationship. Proof can come in several forms, such as a tax return showing you filed jointly and claimed that you were married, or paperwork claiming one as a dependent covered under the other's employer health insurance. Even small things like anniversary cards can help to prove a common law marriage existed. When a couple gets married after living together for several years, yet one of them later claims that they had a common law marriage the entire time, this claim can be suspect. In this instance, the courts will question why the couple had a wedding ceremony if they thought they were already married.

If you do not have a common law marriage, your breakup is not governed by family law. Instead, it may be treated simply as a contractual arrangement or partnership, if anything.

Living Together

In the past several decades, the number of people who live to-gether, either instead of or prior to marriage, has grown tremen-dously. According to the U.S. Census Bureau, there were 9.7 million Americans living with an unmarried partner of the opposite sex in the year 2000.[6] It is now slightly more common for a couple to live together prior to marriage than not. One study found that over a five-year period, 55% of opposite-sex couples married at some point after moving in together, 40% eventually broke up, and the rest re-mained living together but unmarried for five years or longer.[7]

Whether moving in together is a gradual process or a planned decision, eventually two residences become one. With their com-bined resources, the couple might move into a nicer home togeth-er, buy furniture and open a joint bank or credit card account. The more financially and materially intertwined the couple becomes, the stickier it gets if they decide to split up. If the couple has chil-dren together, the legal system still has provisions for determin-ing custody and child support, but division of property is much more difficult when you have no divorce procedures to guide you in breaking up.

Children of Unmarried Parents

Along with the increase in the number of people living together and waiting longer to be married has come an increase in the num-ber of children born to unmarried parents. In 2004, more than 35% of the children born in the U.S. were to unmarried women. Only 24% of these children were born to women under 20 years old. The largest number, 59%, were born to women in their twenties.[8] Many of these children will become the subjects of custody battles and conflicts over visitation and child support, if they haven't already.

If you have children without being married, there is no divorce when you separate from your partner, but that doesn't mean you shouldn't legally determine custody at this point. If you don't, it could become an issue later in your child's life. The fact that a child's parents were not married does not guarantee that the mother will get custody. Judges primarily consider what is best for the children in deciding this important issue. Fathers sometimes gain custody and so do grandparents.

Under the Texas Family Code, a man is legally presumed to be the child's father if:

- The child was born during a marriage or within 300 days after the termination of the marriage; or
- After the child was born, the father married the mother and he either:
   o Filed an assertion of paternity with the Bureau of Vital Statistics; or
   o Was voluntarily named as the father on the child's birth certificate; or
   o Promised on record to support the child as his own; or
- During the first two years of the child's life, he continuously lived in the same household as the child and told other people that the child was his.

A presumed father automatically has all the rights and duties of a parent unless the mother successfully challenges his paternity. The father's parental rights and duties may also be legally established by a written acknowledgment of paternity signed by both parents and filed with the Bureau of Vital Statistics, by a court order establishing his paternity following a paternity suit or by his adoption of the child.

Statistics show that over the years, children from conventional marriages receive far more child support, on average, than those from unmarried parents. When a man denies that he is the father of a child, proving paternity can be essential to getting child support. In years past, blood tests could prove that a man was *not* the father but could not establish with any certainty that he was the father. Today, DNA testing establishes paternity to a 99.9% probability. Though DNA testing is more often used on behalf of the mother, men can also utilize this science to establish or deny their paternity in contested cases.

Palimony in Texas

The word palimony is derived from the words "pal" and "alimony." It's essentially the same thing as alimony but is the term used when a couple was never married. Although palimony doesn't exist as a legal principle in Texas, that doesn't mean people haven't tried to collect it. In 1990, tennis star Martina Navratilova was sued in a Fort Worth court by her live-in lover, Judy Nelson, for violation of their palimony agreement. Ms. Nelson's attorney contended that the two women had made a binding contract and presented a video that showed Ms. Navratilova promising to love and care for Ms. Nelson.

In order for a contract to be legally binding, each person has to provide something of value. For example, one partner might agree to do all the laundry if the other agrees to pay the electric bill. Each person must also deal in good faith and the agreement cannot violate the law. Ms. Navratilova's attorney argued that, among other things, the something of value provided by Ms. Nelson was sex, which amounted to prostitution, an illegal activity. The case was settled before it could go to trial, so the legal principles argued by the defense were never tested in court.

Palimony has been tested numerous times — in both straight and gay relationships in Texas and around the country — against film actor Lee Marvin, Playboy founder Hugh Hefner, pianist Van Cliburn and others. Most palimony cases — especially those involving famous people — settle out of court, since the threat of adverse publicity may more compelling than the legal principles involved.

Annulment

An annulment essentially cancels out a marriage as if it never happened. Its intent is to dissolve a union that you might not have entered into if you'd had all the facts in the first place. The record shows that while numerous couples with "buyer's remorse" try to gain an annulment after a hasty marriage, few couples actually qualify.

In most cases where an annulment is granted, the marriage typically has not lasted for more than a few weeks or months. Therefore, you have not usually had time to acquire assets and debts together or conceive children, which makes much of the divorce process unnecessary.

Typical reasons why you might request an annulment include wanting to avoid the stigma of divorce, avoiding the 60-day waiting period and having a legitimate reason why the marriage should not have occurred in the first place. The one difficulty in asking for an annulment is that you have to prove your reasons. If you cannot, you'll have to dissolve your marriage through the usual divorce process.

The basic grounds for an annulment in Texas are:

- Underage marriage
- Under the influence of alcohol or narcotics at the time of the ceremony
- Impotency
- Fraud, duress, or force
- Mental incapacity
- A divorce within 30 days prior to the ceremony
- Ceremony less than 72 hours after marriage license issued

If you think one of the above situations applies to your marriage, time is of the essence. In almost every case, you must cease to live with your spouse as soon as possible after realizing your situation or you must act on the information within a short period of time. If you discover the problem, try to make the marriage work anyway and then finally give up, you may no longer qualify for an annulment. If you do not act immediately, your only option may be to get a divorce, even if the initial circumstances of the marriage may have qualified for an annulment.

Most annulments are granted on the grounds of fraud. For example, your spouse may not disclose a felony record or may knowingly lie about the ability to conceive children. If you think fraud or any of the other situations mentioned above may apply to you, contact an attorney as soon as possible to discuss the exact requirements and the procedure for getting an annulment.

5

Family Violence

DOMESTIC VIOLENCE IS THE PRIMARY CAUSE of injury to women between the ages of 15 and 44 in America — more than car accidents, muggings, and rapes combined. Each year more than two million women in this country report being beaten by a spouse or partner.[9] Contrary to popular belief, men also suffer from domestic violence, and in numbers that are increasing.

"Tensions associated with divorce may increase incidents of physical violence," says Dr. Richard Warshak, clinical psychologist and author of *Divorce Poison: Protecting the Parent-Child Bond from a Vindictive Ex*. "It's important to differentiate between violence that is chronic versus situational. If the violence is situational and happens only once, your job is to shield your children and get help. If the violence is ongoing, that is a completely different problem that must be dealt with accordingly."

An abusive spouse may intimidate the other parent by saying that if he or she leaves, that parent's relationship with the kids is over. "It is important not to be passive in the face of this behavior," says Dr. Warshak, "because your children desperately need you."

Young children are defenseless in these situations, but teenage boys can face an even greater danger. Studies have found that the leading cause of injury to 14-year-old boys involves putting themselves between batterers and their mothers, and that the majority of young men between the ages of 11 and 20 who are serving prison time for homicide killed their mother's abusers.[10]

Often the first step in ending the abuse is to admit that it is occurring and is not your fault. The second and most important step is to get help and take yourself out of the situation. Once you and your children are safe, you should gather evidence of the abuse so that your attorney can prove it in court. Evidence can include photos, witnesses and reports by medical personnel and police.

If you are an abuser or feel that you are losing control and may become an abuser, there are support groups and therapy that can help you change your behavior. Learning to control your anger and your actions may enable you to save your relationship and your family.

Alleging Abuse in a Divorce Proceeding

In the late 1980s, the assumption that the mother should always be granted custody of the children, except in extreme circumstances, began to fade. Courts began considering and awarding custody to fathers more often, so industrious attorneys concocted a new strategy to prevent this. Many of them claimed that the fathers abused the children. The mere allegation of abuse was enough to cut a father off from his kids and endanger his very freedom. In some cases the abuse was real, but in others it was simply an example of using a hot-button issue to gain favorable settlement terms.

Today, judges and juries have heard child abuse claims in conjunction with divorce so many times that rather than assuming it's true, they become suspicious and look for proof. The parents under the most scrutiny are those who make their first allegation of physical or sexual abuse immediately after a divorce complaint has been filed. In these cases, the courts want to know why the abused spouse has not come forward before. If you or your children are being abused, do not let this attitude stop you. Physical and emotional abuse is scary and often carries threats so that you will not tell anyone. Professionals know this and can help you through this process. Just be aware that since so many parents lie about abuse, legitimate cases must now meet a higher standard of proof. More specifically, judges are adamant that you provide compelling evidence.

Signs of Physical Abuse

Physical abuse in any form damages everyone involved. Children especially carry the emotional scars of surviving abuse well into adulthood, even when the abuse was not directed at them but at a parent. It is important to recognize the signs, because the added strain of a divorce can push an abuser over the edge from threatening to acting.

Signs that physical abuse is happening or may be imminent include:

- Screaming and threatening another person
- Breaking dishes and other objects when angry
- Forcing someone to commit sexual acts
- Threatening to hurt someone for leaving the relationship
- Threatening someone with guns, knives or other weapons
- Hitting, kicking, slapping or pushing

If any of these are happening to you, take action immediately to protect yourself and your children. If you feel threatened, leave the situation. Stay with family members, friends or in a shelter until you can obtain relief in court. If you leave, do everything possible to take your children with you. Consider contacting the police if your spouse has assaulted you and, as soon as you are able, get professional help to understand your options.

Documenting Abuse

Documenting the abuse is an essential step in your case. Taking photos of your bruised face may be unpleasant, but it is the most powerful evidence you can present at trial.

If possible, evidence should be backed up by the testimony of your doctor or that of police officers who responded to calls at your residence. Doctors and police officers can also direct you to other professional help. Often witnesses such as friends and family can be used.

If a doctor believes your child has suffered physical abuse, state law requires that you report it to Child Protective Services, a branch of the Texas Department of Protective and Regulatory Services. Be aware that this may start a chain reaction you cannot stop, so you must understand the seriousness of your charge. That agency will act according to certain laws and may require that the child be taken away from the dangerous situation. If your child needs medical attention, do not hesitate to get help, but if you simply want to have your child evaluated by a professional in preparation for a divorce, it can be wise to first seek legal advice.

Involving the Authorities

When abuse against you or your children escalates, it's usually a good idea to call the police. If you can leave, do so and then call from a safe location. If the police believe they have enough evidence, they can arrest your spouse on the spot. Many people who call the police are reluctant to press charges against their abusers. This response frustrates the police and may cause them to question your motives.

Whether you press charges or not, the incident will generate a police report that provides a written record you can use in your defense stating what the police witnessed at the scene. If you press charges, be patient. It is a lengthy and involved process that usually requires you to testify about the offense before a magistrate in the jurisdiction where the abuse occurred. Next, they'll issue a warrant, and once the police arrest your spouse, the case will be set for trial. If it is a first offense, the court may order counseling rather than jail time. After repeated incidents, the court will put your spouse in jail.

Even though it is hard to press charges against someone you love (or fear), you must document the person's behavior to receive protection. If you do not seek help, the problem could escalate into a potentially fatal incident. According to a 2005 survey of the Bureau of Justice Statistics, a program of the U.S. Department of Justice, each year approximately 22% of solved murders are committed by a family member. Domestic violence can happen in any family regardless of gender, race, religion or lifestyle.

Protective Orders

An ex parte protective order is issued without the presence of your spouse or his or her attorney. It can be issued in an emergency to protect you or your children from continued family violence. A protective order can force the other spouse from the home without a contested hearing if you sign an affidavit that gives a detailed description of the family violence that has just occurred and appear in person to testify at an ex parte hearing.

Three conditions must exist for the judge to order your spouse from your home without advance notice. They are as follows:

1. You must have lived at the residence within the last 30 days;
2. There must be clear evidence that your spouse has committed family violence during the same time period; and
3. There must be a clear and present danger that your spouse will likely commit further family violence.

Since an ex parte protective order is only valid for 20 days, the judge or magistrate who considers the application will schedule a hearing during that time to determine if a final protective order should be issued. To issue the order at the hearing, the court must decide whether family violence has occurred and is likely to occur in the future.

A protective order is a serious document that elicits a quick police response if it is violated. Violation of a protective order is a Class A misdemeanor unless the defendant has been convicted two or more times or has violated the protective order by stalking or assaulting you. In this event, the offense is a much more serious third-degree felony.

Generally a protective order will last two years. The court may require your spouse to complete a batterer's intervention and prevention program, attend counseling or perform other acts. In addition, a protective order may prohibit your spouse from communicating with anyone protected by the order or going near your residence or place of employment or business or harassing or following you or your children.

Educating Parents

Over the years, the public perception of what constitutes child abuse has changed dramatically. What was once considered corporal punishment is now seen as abuse by many in the social science community. Similarly, the actions and fights that take place between parents during a divorce are increasingly thought to be a form of child abuse. This attitude has created a nationwide trend of educating parents, with the goal of lessening the trauma children endure as a result of divorce.

In response to family violence, many courts order batterers to undergo intervention and prevention programs, anger management therapy, individual counseling or other types of aggressive therapy.

Certain family court judges also recommend or routinely mandate parenting classes out of concern for the well-being of the children. These classes teach parents the effects of divorce on children and techniques for parenting during this time.

In Dallas, several programs like this are in operation, including those sponsored by the Child & Family Guidance Center and the CAP Center (Child Abuse Prevention Center). Many other counties across Texas have similar programs.

Appendix F (page 279) lists a number of hotlines and other resources.

What You Gonna Believe: Me or Your Lyin' Ears?

"People sometimes misjudge the way a jury will view evidence. In a child custody trial where I represented the father, the two sides were fairly even until the other side introduced tape recordings made by the wife of conversations between herself and her husband. She thought they would show what a sorry guy he was. The recordings did convey a message, but it wasn't the one she planned.

"Instead, the recordings showed the jury what a difficult person she was. After we won, I polled the jury and they confirmed that the tape recordings — which the other side had considered their smoking gun — were the most compelling evidence in favor of my client."

Kevin Fuller
Family Law Attorney

Part Two:
Preparing Your Case

6

Collaborative Law: Following a New Pathway

DIVORCE COURTS HAVE HISTORICALLY fostered aggressive behavior and needless suffering. The opposing parties went to war, while their attorneys attempted to punish the other side. It worked that way during the 1970s and early 80s—when divorce was most prevalent—and everyone who divorced had to endure the conflict because there was no real alternative to litigation.

During the 1990s, family law experts who were frustrated with the destructive nature of divorce litigation developed a new approach known as collaborative law. This is a radical departure from the traditional methods of dealing with divorce. Collaborative law is often compared with mediation, but while mediation is a dispute resolution method used in conjunction with litigation, collaborative law is a separate process that represents a complete transformation in the way a divorcing couple and their attorneys relate to each other. Ideally, collaborative law participants never see the inside of a courtroom.

Spouses who want to maintain a positive relationship after the divorce can now use collaborative law. The most likely collaborative law participants at this early stage in the development of the process include couples with children, those who own or operate a family business, those who share the same workplace or those who have a large group of mutual friends.

Collaborative law is designed to resolve disputes while keeping each person's personal and financial dignity intact. In this process, harmony is more important than vengeance. Collaborative law is strictly voluntary, although some Texas judges are beginning to recommend it in certain situations.

A Novel Approach

Unlike mediation where you and your spouse are in separate rooms, the collaborative process brings the parties face to face, usually in the office of one of the attorneys. Rather than one marathon session, meetings are normally two hours in length and follow an agenda created jointly by the attorneys. Cases can settle in as few as four meetings, although the more complicated cases usually take much longer.

"The process is not driven by negotiation as much as by goals," says Dallas family lawyer Kevin Fuller, whose practice is increasingly moving toward the collaborative model. "It works better because people attack the problem instead of each other. By focusing on the different interests and concerns of each party, a win-win resolution can be more easily discovered than by focusing on what a court or jury will do with a certain set of facts."

The collaborative process works through these five basic steps:

1. Laying ground rules and organizing
2. Establishing goals, interests and concerns
3. Gathering information
4. Brainstorming options and solutions

5. Evaluating the options and selecting the ones that meet as many goals as possible

The first three steps carry a low emotional impact. Step four is where the real work begins. "That's where you find out if the case is going to be easy or hard," says Fuller. "About half of all collaborative cases come up with good solutions in step four and settle without any problem."

Participation Agreement

Once you and your spouse agree to use collaborative law, the attorneys sign a participation agreement that commits all of you to the process. All parties agree to abide by a certain code of conduct that includes full disclosure of information to the other side even without being asked and not negotiating outside the scheduled meetings.

The following paragraph, taken from the Collaborative Law Participation Agreement approved by The Collaborative Law Institute of Texas, contains the essence of that agreement:

> *We adopt this conflict resolution process, which relies on honesty, cooperation, integrity and professionalism geared toward the future well-being of the restructured family. Our goal is to eliminate the negative economic, social and emotional consequences of litigation. We commit to the collaborative law process to resolve the parties' differences with the goal of achieving a resolution that is acceptable to both parties under the circumstances.*

Fuller believes that just "having these rules and discussing them between the parties helps to significantly diffuse the emotional atmosphere at the negotiating table."

Expectations of Conduct in Collaborative Law

The following list describes the conduct expected of the spouses who have agreed to use the collaborative process. This list is provided by the Dallas Alliance of Collaborative Professionals, a practice group of non-affiliated attorneys trained to work with participants in the collaborative process.

1. Participants will focus on the future and avoid unnecessary discussions of the past.
2. Participants will focus on resolving conflict and not on assessing blame.
3. Participants will listen carefully to the goals that begin every four-way meeting, and will take actions and make decisions in furtherance of the shared goals.
4. Participants will address the others in a courteous manner and tone. Participants will not interrupt when another person is speaking. Participants will avoid sarcastic, contemptuous, critical, defensive or judgmental communication and comments.
5. If the participant feels progress has ceased or that he or she is about to lose control and say or do something to impede progress, the participant will call for a break. If the break is insufficient to calm the affected participant, the meeting may be terminated.
6. Each participant will speak only for himself or herself. Participants will use "I" instead of "you" sentences.
7. Participants will express their true interests.
8. Participants will be patient with each other and their lawyers. All participants will assume that each participant is acting in good faith and realize that not everyone moves at the same pace. To pull together, each participant must sometimes accommodate by slowing down. Delays in the

collaborative law process can happen with everyone acting in good faith.

9. Participants will follow the agenda for each four-way meeting. If there are other topics that a participant wants to address, he or she will ask that it be included in the agenda for the next four-way meeting.

10. Participants will be honest.

Role of Attorneys

A collaborative law attorney is specially trained in this area of family law and has an entirely different focus than he or she would have in mediation or litigation. "One of the biggest challenges a lawyer faces in the litigation process is trying to wear two hats at one time," says Fuller. "It is hard to both fully prepare for trial and keep everyone relatively calm to pursue settlement options."

In the collaborative process, attorneys have one goal of finding the best possible solutions for you. Your attorney can focus solely on achieving the best settlement because he or she does not need to worry about taking the case to trial. The participation agreement states that if the collaborative process fails, your attorney cannot represent you at trial. You would need to find a new attorney and start over. This strategy helps attorneys become more cooperative and invested in reaching a settlement.

A Team of Neutral Experts

Many experts advocate a team approach to collaborative law. The team often consists of six people: the divorcing parties, their attorneys, a mental health professional and a financial expert. Your attorneys choose the experts jointly so they are neutral and can offer solutions from objective points of view with benefits for both of you. "It's faster and less expensive to start out with the team approach," says Fuller. "The process is more likely to run into trouble without that approach, and then you have to work harder to get everyone back on track once you've brought in the experts to fix it."

The mental health professional helps you navigate the emotional minefield in which you find yourself. This person serves as both referee and communications facilitator. When one spouse gets emotional or lashes out, the mental health professional steps in and helps to keep communications safe and constructive.

"Lawyers have little or no formal training in how to help people deal with overwhelming emotions," says Fuller. "They often have no idea how to respond to those emotions, so a mental health professional fills this role." Since these experts do not testify in court for or against either spouse, their constructive approach fosters an environment of cooperation rather than blame.

The financial expert is usually a financial planner or certified divorce planner. This expert is in charge of gathering financial information and verifying its accuracy. During the process, this person does basic financial planning and shows a divorcing couple their best options in each case. This neutral voice can be very helpful since a suggestion from the other side may be viewed with suspicion.

Multiple Benefits

Collaborative law carries many possible benefits, including the following:

More privacy

Since the collaborative process is handled outside the courtroom and without depositions or document requests, the amount of information filed on record and made public is significantly reduced.

Better communication

Rather than getting settlement offers and other information second or third hand, you work directly with your spouse and his or her attorney, which cuts down on confusion. If a mental health professional is part of the team, that person works to ensure that everyone speaks constructively and that each side hears what the other has to say.

Lower fees

Litigation is time consuming and expensive. Collaborative law aims to streamline the process and can lower the cost of divorce, although there is no guarantee of that in all cases. Sharing experts saves money, and you may need fewer experts since the tone is more cooperative and less confrontational. With mediation, an attorney still has to prepare for trial, but since this is not true in collaborative law, you do not need to pay your attorney for time spent on trial preparation unless settlement fails.

Better atmosphere

You can call for a break at any time during a meeting if you feel that emotions are running too high or you're just not ready for the next step. After a break, if you still don't feel up to it, you can end the meeting and schedule the next one. This is a much more relaxed atmosphere than in a trial, where stopping and starting again is very difficult to accomplish. An atmosphere of cooperation, where calm, productive discussions are encouraged, creates a better foundation for working with your spouse in the future, especially if you share children.

Better schedule

The schedule of meetings is completely up to the parties and their attorneys. It is more collegial. You do not have to worry about showing up prepared for court, only to find that a more pressing case takes precedence over yours and will be heard by the judge that day instead of your case. Nor will a judge schedule a court appearance in the middle of someone's vacation or important business meeting.

Better for children

In collaborative law, you can enlist neutral experts to assist you in determining custody and other issues regarding your children. Because these experts cannot testify in court, you to be less likely to become defensive and lay blame. Instead of trying to prove that your spouse is bad and you are good, the two of you can focus on finding solutions that will benefit your children the most.

These benefits are all factors to consider when deciding whether the collaborative process is right for you.

When it Doesn't Work

Collaborative law does not always work successfully, just as mediation and litigation have their failures, too. The collaborative process can be extremely difficult when one spouse is too emotionally distraught to negotiate, wants to punish the other spouse or is psychologically incapable of participating in the process. Collaborative law works well for two emotionally healthy and mature individuals.

Having a mental health professional present can improve negative situations but may not always be enough. Abusive spouses and spouses who suffer from a mental illness such as narcissism often have difficulty working through the process in good faith.

When one spouse wants to punish the other, litigation may become inevitable. "Sometimes in collaborative law the spouse who is at fault agrees to give more than his or her fair share," says Fuller, "and still the other side won't accept the deal. So the process is halted and goes to court. In the end, the wounded spouse ends up with less money but gets to publicly punish the ex in court."

Finding a Collaborative Lawyer

Many collaborative lawyers practice in groups of independent, unaffiliated legal professionals, because two attorneys who are familiar with each other and properly trained in collaborative law do a better job with these cases. You can find collaborative law practice groups in most urban areas of Texas.

If you're interested in exploring the possibility of a collaborative law divorce, check out the web sites of the Collaborative Law Institute of Texas (www.collablawtexas.com) and the International Academy of Collaborative Professionals (www.collaborativepractice.com). Both sites contain additional information on the collaborative process and can help you find an attorney trained in this field. Some lawyers who handle cases collaboratively are not members of practice groups, so if you live in a smaller town or rural area, seek information from lawyers near you.

7

Shaping an Uncontested Divorce

A TRULY UNCONTESTED DIVORCE is rare and beautiful. It means that two people who agree on very little in a marriage — to the point of pulling the plug on the whole thing — can come together and say goodbye gracefully. Divorce brings out the worst in people more often than it brings out the best. So you should protect yourself in case your divorce starts out cordially but takes a turn for the worse.

In the case of Maxine and Gregory, she assumed from the start that their divorce would be uncontested. She knew exactly what property she wanted from the marriage and she didn't worry about what Gregory wanted. He had always been the passive one in the relationship, so she had no reason to believe he would behave differently during the divorce. When Maxine went to see her lawyer, she wanted to know the fees for an uncontested divorce, telling him, "All we need is for you to prepare the papers."

Gregory was fine with this at the start, just as Maxine said. But then he began talking to his friends and family members who advised him to stand up for himself, and soon he started speaking up like never before. Ego, jealousy, anger and resentment came out during discussions about custody and property. Eventually they began to say things they couldn't take back and their uncontested divorce went out the window. From then on, their divorce was contested and, therefore, became expensive.

Keeping Conflict to a Minimum

It is important to stand up for yourself. But to keep conflict to a minimum, learn how to restrain yourself if you feel the need to lash out in anger or revenge. Sometimes keeping your mouth shut is the only way to keep feelings in check. Otherwise, once the floodgates open, it's hard to stop the words that escalate between you and your spouse. Many agreements get derailed before the papers can be executed when one of you says something inflammatory. There are good reasons to nullify agreements, but pride and ego are not among them.

Preparing the Correct Documents

You must prepare certain documents in all divorces, contested or not, and present them to the judge and the other side. The one who files for divorce is called the petitioner, and the opposing party is called the respondent. You must file the petition and the proof of notice to the respondent with the court and the judge must sign the decree of divorce. If the divorce becomes contested at any time, other documents may be necessary.

Petition

When people say they have filed for divorce, the petition is the document that accomplishes that act. It contains certain factual information about you, your spouse and your children, and lists the grounds for the divorce. A petitioner files the petition and has it served on the respondent by having it hand-delivered by an authorized process server. In Texas, the no-fault ground for divorce is insupportability, which means the legitimate ends of the marriage relationship have been destroyed by discord or conflict of personalities and this condition is irreconcilable. There are other grounds for divorce including mental cruelty and adultery, but since Texas allows no-fault divorce, you are not required to list these other reasons.

Answer

The respondent replies by filing an answer to the petition. You must file your answer no later than 10 AM on the Monday immediately following the expiration of 20 days after the date the petition is served on you. If you do not file your answer by this deadline, the petitioner can get orders signed by the judge without your knowledge or consent.

Inventory

This is a detailed listing of your assets and liabilities, which may contain account numbers and other personal financial information. Sometimes this document is filed with the court, but since it becomes public record, the court may not require you to file it or may allow you to use partial account numbers.

Decree of Divorce

This document, which the trial judge signs at the end of the process, grants the divorce, contains orders concerning any children and divides the property. The decree can approve a separate settlement agreement called an agreement incident to divorce and make it binding on both of you. Alternatively, it may contain the full agreement you have put together, which dispenses with the need for the separate document.

The judge must wait a minimum of 60 days from the time you file the petition before granting the divorce, to ensure that neither you nor your spouse has moved too quickly and to allow ample time if you are considering reconciliation. Once there is an agreement and all the documents are prepared properly, only one of you has to appear in court. There the judge signs the decree and declares you legally divorced.

Be aware that there is a 30-day waiting period after the decree is signed before you can legally remarry. Since divorces can take a long time, many people are already waiting to remarry and have planned weddings to take place as soon as the court issues the divorce decree. A judge can waive the 30-day waiting period under certain circumstances, but to avoid having to cancel a wedding you should wait until after the 30 days have passed.

Remaining Friends with Your Spouse

In an uncontested divorce, you are more likely to remain on speaking terms with your spouse. If that is your goal, decide how important this cordiality is before you begin negotiations, and talk about it with your attorney. You may have to compromise and give up things you want, so you need to decide how much you are willing to concede to keep the relationship civil. This is much more important, of course, if you have children together.

Before you begin the divorce process, an emotionally disinterested third party (an attorney) with experience handling divorce matters can help you navigate and avoid costly mistakes. It's a good idea to have a divorce expert assess your situation and then inform you about your rights and options.

You are under no obligation to file for divorce just because you speak with an attorney. Over the years, we've had a few clients meet with us to evaluate their legal situation but remain married. The more you know, the easier it is to make good decisions and keep calm when negotiating with your spouse.

When Your Spouse Is Suddenly the Enemy

There comes a time in many divorces when communication breaks down and progress comes to a halt. This usually happens when you least expect it, in the midst of negotiations that were going well. At this point, you may need help to reach a resolution. If you are not already working with an experienced attorney, find one who will help you work toward your goals.

Once your divorce becomes contested, your spouse becomes the opposition, if only for the duration of the divorce. You may not want it that way, but these are the cards you are dealt and it is important to focus on what is in your hand.

8

The Preparation Stage

THE PHRASE "PEACE THROUGH STRENGTH" was part of our national strategy during the Cold War, and it may hint at a good tactic during a contested divorce. In this case, your strength is preparation and information. Work with your attorney to prepare and handle your case as if it will go to trial. If settlement efforts fail, at least you'll be ready.

It's rare to do much preparation before you even file for divorce, but we recall a case where a man did just that. He carefully planned the breakup of his marriage for nearly a year before making his intentions known to his wife. He wanted custody of his young son, because he thought his wife was mentally unstable. We were convinced that the man was sincere, and that he wasn't just on a power trip. It was never his intention to keep the mother and son apart, but to control the boy's whereabouts for the child's sake. And so he spent a year painstakingly documenting her eccentricities, her lack of involvement in their son's life and her inattention to the needs of their family. All of his planning paid off when the court awarded him sole custody.

Assertive — though not aggressive — action gives you the best chance to achieve a divorce you can live with. Talk to your attorney about the things you value and how you can protect them. If your spouse abuses you or your children, let your attorney advise you on the best course of action. Your attorney has to know what problems need to be solved. Otherwise, he or she cannot help you get what you want or need.

Temporary Restraining Orders

A common procedural device used in family law cases is a temporary restraining order (TRO), a court order that restrains or prevents someone from doing certain things to the person who requested the order or to property owned by both parties. If the petitioner (the one who filed for divorce) requests a TRO, it is granted automatically as long as it only contains the standard restrictions.

The following is an abbreviated list of those standard restrictions in a TRO issued during a divorce. It prevents one or both spouses from engaging in these acts:

- Using profane or threatening language either verbally or in writing
- Making repeated or anonymous phone calls
- Causing bodily injury
- Destroying, removing or concealing property
- Falsifying records relating to property
- Misrepresenting or refusing to disclose the existence, amount or location of property
- Selling, transferring, assigning, mortgaging or encumbering property
- Incurring any debts, other than legal expenses in connection with the case
- Making withdrawals or borrowing funds from checking, savings or other bank accounts

- Entering safe-deposit boxes
- Changing or altering the beneficiaries on life insurance policies
- Canceling, altering or failing to renew or pay premiums for any insurance policies
- Opening or diverting mail addressed to the spouse or children
- Terminating or limiting the spouse's credit or charge cards
- Discontinuing or reducing withholdings for federal income taxes
- Destroying, disposing or altering any financial records
- Destroying, disposing or altering any e-mail or other electronic data relevant to the case
- Terminating or affecting the service of utilities at the family residence
- Excluding the spouse from the family residence
- Entering, operating or exercising control over the spouse's vehicle
- Disturbing the peace of the children
- Withdrawing the children from school
- Hiding the children from the spouse
- Making disparaging remarks about the spouse in front of the children
- Being intoxicated while caring for the children
- Letting a boyfriend or girlfriend sleep over when the children are present

A TRO is only in effect for 14 days, so the court must set a hearing for temporary orders within that time period. If the case cannot be heard within 14 days, the court will normally extend the TRO for an additional 14 days so that it does not expire while you are waiting for the hearing. At the hearing, the court decides whether to continue the TRO as a temporary injunction until the final decree of divorce is issued, and whether to add additional restrictions or modify it in some other way to accommodate special circumstances.

Other Temporary Orders

While the TRO or temporary injunction says what you can't do, other temporary orders add to the restrictions a list of things you must do. Standard items covered by temporary orders include requirements to:

- Prepare an inventory of all property
- Pay temporary child support
- Pay temporary spousal support
- Produce documents
- Pay interim attorney fees
- Pay other specific debts

The temporary orders may also:

- Appoint parents as conservators of the children
- Provide visitation with children
- Award temporary use of property, including homes and automobiles

Premarital Agreements

Reversing the terms of a premarital agreement, known as "breaking a prenup," is difficult if the agreement is written properly. People use prenups to protect assets they held prior to getting married or that they receive during the marriage. Prenups are especially beneficial for assets that are not easily divisible, such as an interest in a family- owned business or a real estate development.

In Texas, the assets owned by you or your spouse before you got married are protected as separate property even without a prenup.

The same applies to assets received by gift or inheritance. Under most conditions, separate property and any appreciation on it are not subject to division. However, income derived from that asset is considered community property unless you have a prenup stating otherwise.

If you or your spouse signed a prenup before you got married, provide a copy of it to your attorney and talk about any concerns you have regarding it. Your attorney will then determine how it will factor into your divorce proceedings.

Be an Information Magnet

Married couples usually have one spouse who makes the majority of the money, pays the bills and keeps the records. This is the documented spouse. The other spouse often has little to do with family finances. This second (undocumented) spouse is at a distinct disadvantage at the beginning of a divorce case. Regardless of which one you are, now is the time to think of yourself as an information magnet. Information can make or break your case. Gather this evidence as early as possible and go over it with your attorney so that your spouse cannot spring it on you at trial or hide it from you.

The information you'll want to gather usually includes three to five years of the following:

- Personal and business tax returns
- Checking, savings and other investment or bank account statements
- Paid bills and invoices
- Stock and bond certificates
- Mortgage and home equity statements
- Credit card statements
- Long-distance telephone bills
- Cellular telephone bills
- Medical records

- Health insurance policies
- Life insurance policies
- Family photos
- Photo evidence of extramarital affairs
- Love letters or other communications between your spouse and a third party
- Evidence of any other secrets that you or your spouse have

Do not destroy this documentation. You merely want to put it away for safekeeping. These documents may or may not be pertinent during settlement negotiations or in a trial, but you'll want to have the opportunity to make that decision. Obtaining this information does not assure you of winning the majority of the marital assets or gaining custody of your children. The facts of your case will dictate how this information is used, either by you or against you, but when your attorney knows all the facts, he or she has a better chance of controlling the situation.

Hidden Assets

Hiding assets isn't just for the wealthy. Anyone can have a rainy day account on the side that is not mentioned in the divorce proceedings. When your spouse hides money from you, you can usually find out about it, although you may need to hire an expert to do so. If you believe your spouse is hiding money, try to get an idea of how much. Otherwise, you risk spending more to find it than it's worth. Bank statements, canceled checks and tax returns can all contain clues to hidden assets. "People hide money in all kinds of creative ways," says Jim Wingate, CPA and family law attorney. "They think certain things can't be traced. But almost anything can be found, even if it takes a subpoena to get it."

One woman began hiding money at the beginning of her marriage. Without her husband's knowledge, she opened a joint account with her father and deposited nearly half of the checks from her small side business into it. During the divorce, the husband did not discover the account until he reviewed a canceled check the woman had written to her father. The memo line said the check was for reimbursement of wedding expenses, yet the husband knew the father was well off and would not have let his daughter reimburse him.

Spying, Sneaking and Snooping

Information obtained through investigation can become crucial evidence in your divorce case. Household and cellphone records are great examples of this. If your spouse tells the judge he or she is practically broke, providing the court with pages of phone calls to some mystery number could refute that claim. The calls could reveal an affair, a bookie or a drug connection. Any of these could explain where your spouse's money goes each month.

The best divorce lawyers in a contested case facing litigation request both personal and business long-distance and cellphone records for the past three to five years, because sometimes people hide these types of activities behind business accounts. Threatening to tell the employer may encourage the guilty spouse to cooperate.

Hiring a Private Investigator

If you impulsively hire a private investigator without consulting your attorney, you may waste valuable time and money. Your attorney probably has an investigator he or she trusts and can recommend. Sometimes the information uncovered by the investigator can make or break your case, so it is essential to hire someone who will gather it correctly.

In one case, an investigator videotaped a mother having sex in a car with someone who was not her husband. While this is what you call solid proof of trashiness, the most damning part of this incident was that her baby son was sitting next to them in a car seat.

Not all evidence uncovered by investigators is so compelling. Often, an investigator's report simply backs up evidence you already have.

Private investigators usually charge by the hour plus any expenses they incur. Their fees are not included in the retainer you pay to your attorney and are often paid up front or as the work is complete. Whatever the results, these services are expensive, and there is no guarantee that you can use what the investigator finds to your advantage. A skilled family law specialist can usually discredit an investigator's report, especially if there are flaws in the actions taken or the investigator lacks experience. You get what you pay for, so if you're going to go to the trouble of hiring an investigator, have your attorney hire a competent one.

Using Video or Audio Evidence

You may think that if you capture your spouse's bad behavior on a video or audio recording, you have all the evidence you need to turn things in your favor. But before you start acting like a spy, get the facts so that you do not wind up in deep trouble. In Texas, at least one party to a conversation must know he or she is being taped. In other words, you can tape yourself talking to your spouse, but it is a criminal offense to wiretap or tape a conversation between your spouse and someone else if neither of them knows they are being recorded.

Although nanny cams have become popular for catching people in the act, don't set one up in your house without your spouse's knowledge. By law, this is considered an invasion of privacy and can subject you to civil liability. You can only video people without their knowledge in places where they do not have a reasonable expectation of privacy, such as a public place. You can record people through the window of a house, car, or hotel room as long as you do so from far enough away that a neighbor or someone walking by could see the same thing you do. You cannot hide in the bushes and put the camera up to the window, because people walking by wouldn't do that. In addition, under no circumstances can you video someone without their knowledge in the seclusion of a bedroom or bathroom without risking liability for invading their privacy.

Even if you follow the law, recording your spouse may not be as helpful as you think. Judges and juries can look at your recording as a devious form of spying. If the evidence you record is not particularly damaging, the judge or jury might punish you for it instead of your spouse. If your spouse continually denies things you know he or she has done, however, a recording may be the only way to prove it. Your attorney can help you decide if the video or audio evidence you gather will help or hurt you.

Keeping Your Attorney Informed

An experienced attorney and a helpful client is a powerful combination. The only way for you and your attorney to work together effectively is to be totally honest with each other. You need to learn to trust your attorney with any information you have about your case. Anything you tell your attorney as part of your case is privileged and must be kept confidential by that attorney, unless it is in furtherance of a crime or fraud and must be made public.

Conversely, your attorney counts on your truthfulness and needs to know that any suspicions you have about your spouse are not simply flights of fancy. If you suspect something about your spouse, tell your attorney. He or she will know whether the information is useful and how to prove it if necessary.

You may have trouble talking about your own secrets, but your attorney needs to know the whole truth. No one is perfect, and it's likely that whatever secrets you harbor, your attorney has heard them all before. Knowing this doesn't make confession any easier. "Truth is a process, not an event," says Dr. Jan DeLipsey, a psychologist who specializes in social sciences and litigation consulting. If you've been covering up lies of current or past behavior, she says, your reflex is to keep covering.

"Lawyers instruct people to just tell the truth," says Dr. De-Lipsey, "but it's not that simple. You have to encourage people to be truthful. Most people need time to learn trust and prepare to tell the truth in front of others. It's hard to trust someone you've only known for a few minutes."

You may have to testify at some point about your mistakes under oath, so begin the process of telling the truth with your attorney. Once your attorney knows your secrets, he or she can help protect you. If the opposition catches your attorney by surprise during a trial or deposition, your case will be much more difficult. Everyone makes mistakes, but if you lie about it under oath, the fact that you lied is usually viewed more harshly than the behavior you attempted to cover up.

Adultery is the most common secret uncovered during a divorce. People who engage in affairs think no one will find out. However, they often make careless mistakes. They go to restaurants where they are likely to run into people they know. They write love letters and take photos and leave them in a briefcase or purse. And they buy flowers and lingerie with a credit card. One man wrote checks to pay his girlfriend's bills from the joint checking account he shared with his wife. He was so conditioned to keep the account straight that he even wrote the girlfriend's name and reason for the check in the memo line. When he denied knowing the woman and having an adulterous affair, the checks told a different story.

If you are having an affair, do not try harder to hide it. End it immediately. Eventually, you will probably get caught, either by your spouse or a private investigator. A finding of fault will be reflected in the settlement of your divorce and you may walk away from the marriage with much less than you could have.

You should also understand the strain you put everyone under by continuing an affair, especially if you have children. The law gives parents the benefit of the doubt, asserting that, even in divorce, no one ceases to be a parent. Yet children frequently feel betrayed by, and angry at, the parent who committed the adultery and had a terrible effect on the marriage and their childhood. Remember that you are a parent and that your children will likely carry the psychological effects of your reckless behavior for the rest of their lives. If this happens, at least let them also remember that you were forthright and available to them in this time of crisis.

9

Building a Winning Case

A NOTED JURIST ONCE SAID there are three sides to every divorce case — his side, her side and the truth. That is why the discovery process is so important. Discovery gives you the ability to obtain information from your spouse, and vice versa, concerning the relevant issues in your case. This process involves either formal or informal requests for information. The objective is to level the playing field so that both sides have access to all the information and documentation necessary to resolve the case.

Laura had trouble getting at the truth in her divorce. Her husband ran his own business and did not make it easy for her to determine how much money he made. Hoping to handle the divorce in a civilized manner, Laura repeatedly asked him for more complete financial information. Finally, he gave her income estimates that she considered suspiciously low. He was always polite and promised he would get her the actual documents that proved it, but he never got around to it.

Soon the time came to enter into serious settlement negotiations. She still had not received any documents from him and had to do something to force him to turn over the records. Laura's attorney sent him a letter requesting every check and invoice, as well as a list of his customers and vendors for the past five years. The letter also requested that he bring all of this information to a deposition they had scheduled, which they estimated would take at least one full day. Within four hours of sending the letter, Laura received the documents she originally requested. At this point her attorney rescinded his request for the other information and canceled the deposition.

Exchanging information between two married adults may not seem that difficult. But the formal procedures in a divorce, such as production requests, inventories and interrogatories can quickly result in intense and highly charged debates over access to information. In a hostile divorce, one side may have to force the other to provide even basic information, like checking account statements and tax returns. Your attorney will decide how important each piece of information is to your case, and to what lengths you should go to obtain it. In general, don't agree to begin discussing settlement options until you are fairly confident that you know about all of the assets and liabilities involved in your divorce.

Requests for Disclosure

Requests for disclosure are a formal discovery tool commonly used in a divorce. By law, the list cannot be changed so it is the same in every case.

The list includes:

- Correct names of you and your spouse
- Contact information for any other people or entities who should be involved in your case as a party to the lawsuit
- The legal theories of your case and the general factual bases for your claims or defenses
- If your case includes a separate lawsuit for monetary dam-

ages, the amount and method of calculating those damages

- Contact information for anyone who has knowledge of facts relevant to your case, and a brief statement of their connection with the case
- Information concerning experts who may testify
- Any indemnity and insuring agreements
- Any settlement agreements
- Any witness statements
- Medical records or a release to obtain them, if you allege physical or mental injury and claim damages for that injury
- If your spouse has alleged physical or mental injury and claims damages against you, any medical records and bills you have obtained using a release they furnished
- Contact information for any person who may be designated as a third party legally responsible for any damages claimed

Interrogatories

Interrogatories are another common discovery tool in a divorce proceeding. They are written questions designed to elicit certain facts. You must answer these questions under oath and your attorney must prepare and return the responses within 30 days.

Since interrogatories are issued early in the process, sometimes you can catch the other side unaware of the consequences of an answer. Sometimes you can unearth an outright lie, which a judge or jury will frown on and which can have an impact on your case.

Interrogatories may include questions relating to children, employment, salary information, bank accounts, charge accounts, assets and debts. You may be asked questions about anyone you listed (in response to the requests for disclosure) as having knowledge of your case, and you may be asked to provide a list of the persons you actually expect to call as witnesses. There may also be fault questions pertaining to such activities as drug abuse, spousal abuse or adultery.

If interrogatories are directed at you, discuss them with your attorney to determine the best way to respond. After your initial responses to the interrogatories, you'll need to update your answers as new information becomes available. That must happen no later than 30 days before trial.

Requests for Production of Documents

This request contains specific demands for documents needed for the case. Typically a request for production of documents asks for three to five years of bank statements, tax returns, credit card statements, insurance information and other financial data and documents, including information concerning children and any other types of evidence either side plans to use at trial.

You must provide copies of all documents requested by the opposing side, unless your attorney asserts a valid objection. If you fail to produce a document when requested, you will usually be prevented from using it in court, because the opposing attorney will object to the admission of documents he or she could not examine beforehand. Failure to produce a requested document may also subject you to monetary fines and other penalties.

Requests for Admissions

A request for admissions asks you or your spouse to admit or deny facts in your case, although admissions are not as commonly used today as they were in the past. Your spouse may be asked to stipulate that a piece of property is actually separate property or to admit or deny an extramarital affair. It can be used to confirm the genuineness of a document, such as a deed or a premarital agreement.

You can put a guilty spouse in a delicate position when asking these questions. Admitting adultery, for instance, may concede a fact the opposition might have trouble proving in court. But denying the relationship is risky. If the other side does prove it at trial, the spouse is not only an adulterer but also a liar.

If you fail to answer a request for admissions in a timely manner, the court can view this as confirmation of what was asked. For example, if you fail to respond when asked if you had an affair, your inaction may translate into admitting that you are guilty. Therefore, you cannot simply avoid answering questions without negative consequences.

Depositions

A deposition can be the most confrontational and informative part of the discovery process, since it is taken in person, under oath, and often with your spouse present. Attorneys use depositions to accomplish many things, such as assessing the opposing party and their case, determining how someone will appear on the witness stand, investigating the substance of his or her testimony and pressuring the opposition by giving them a taste of the confrontational atmosphere they can expect at trial.

Before you decide to take the deposition of your estranged spouse or other witnesses, exhaust every effort to reach a settlement and make certain you can use the information. Depositions can inflame an already tense situation and cost from hundreds of dollars to several thousand dollars. If you want to find out about a bank account with a few hundred dollars in it, there are more cost-effective ways to get that information. When you suspect the existence of a large hidden bank account, though, or if custody of your children is at stake, a deposition can be a worthwhile investment.

Usually your deposition takes place in the office of one of the attorneys and in the presence of a court reporter who records everything you say. Depositions are normally limited to six hours, but with breaks, lunch, and other delays and interruptions, they can easily last a full day and sometimes carry over into the next.

After the deposition, the court reporter types up exactly what everyone said and provides a transcript of the entire proceeding. This can later be used to discredit a witness who changes his or her testimony at trial. Therefore, it is important to prepare for the deposition and then obtain a transcript afterwards.

If you give a deposition, your lawyer will be present to protect your rights, but your spouse's attorney leads the deposition and will ask questions about the facts of the case and the history of your marriage. Always tell the truth, but keep in mind that there are numerous strategies for handling a deposition. Your attorney can advise you about the impact of a particular line of questioning and how to respond.

Your deposition may help or hurt your case if you get to trial, depending on how you testify and the particular facts of your case. You must be prepared to name each and every reason why you want the divorce, if you plan to utilize those reasons at trial. As with the requests for disclosure, you may be asked to name every person who has information relevant to your case and describe that information. Work with your attorney to prepare for your deposition so you do not forget critical parts of the case under the pressure and intensity of the moment. You will have an opportunity to correct your testimony after the transcript is typed. But it is always better to minimize corrections, as substantial revisions may look suspicious.

Sometimes a deposition is a shortcut to discovering the opposition's entire case. In one divorce where a large amount of property was at stake, the wife filed a vicious and accusatory pleading alleging wrongdoing by her husband. The husband's attorney knew there was no evidence to back up her claims, so he scheduled a deposition at the very start of the case instead of waiting to complete the other discovery. The deposition revealed there were no facts to support the wife's claims. Her attorney filed the pleading anyway, hoping to put the husband on the defensive. Instead, the exact opposite occurred. The husband put his wife and her attorney on the defensive and they stayed there throughout the case because their tactic failed.

10

Mediation May Be Required

MEDIATION IS THE MOST COMMON FORM of alternative dispute resolution. It encourages communication and compromise instead of conflict. The mediation process has become very popular over the past 20 years, and it's generally less expensive to mediate than to litigate. If you want a relationship with your spouse after the divorce, as parents or as owners of a business, a mediated settlement usually beats the adversarial process of two parties going into court seeking justice by bashing each other.

In her book *The Argument Culture*, linguist Deborah Tannen suggests we need an alternative to the idea that a winner and a loser must emerge from every case that goes to court.[11]

"The American legal system is a prime example of trying to solve problems by pitting two sides against each other and letting them slug it out in public," she writes. "It reflects and reinforces our assumption that truth emerges when two polarized, warring extremes are set against each other."

When Bob and Irene decided to divorce, they argued over the most trivial details. Bob was in the printing business, and they couldn't even agree that some antique books and magazines he had purchased belonged to him. Their attorneys saw their disagreements firsthand. During their one and only settlement conference, the two of them stood across the table like rhinos about to charge. Since that meeting, their attorneys engaged in telephone tag, with Bob calling his attorney, who called Irene's attorney, who called Irene. If she was out, the whole thing worked in reverse until they connected. When another question arose, the whole process started all over again.

While the meter ran on both sides, the attorneys' bills neared six figures and still they had not gone to trial. It soon became clear that if they had any money left when they completed the process, there would likely be so much animosity between them that joint parenting of their children would be impossible. Mediation was created for cases like these.

Explaining the Process

Moving the process away from the courthouse and into a mediator's office can reduce the conflict and tension that occurs in a divorce. An attorney's job in court is to win, but an attorney's job in mediation is to negotiate. The best you can hope for is a fair settlement that holds up over time, and mediation can often accomplish that better, faster, cheaper and with less stress than going to court. "In mediation, you can forge your own destiny," says mediator Rothwell B. Pool. "But at the courthouse, you are absolutely without control. The judge has the final say. If two people work for 30 years to build something together, it's tough to let a third party divide it."

The mediation process begins in one of two ways, depending on the style of the mediator. Either you, your spouse and your representatives—attorneys, accountants, financial planners—start out in separate rooms or simply gather in the same room for an initial joint session while the mediator lays out the ground rules. Then, with the parties disbursed into separate rooms, the mediator begins a day of diplomacy, highlighting points of agreement, attempting to smooth over any disagreements and helping you come up with creative ways to resolve your case.

The best mediators inspire people to work toward common goals and look to the future. "A lot of times mediation is about reaching an agreement you can live with," says family court Judge Marilea Lewis. "It's not going to be ideal. Ideal ended when you decided to file for divorce."

If you reach agreement, the attorneys and the mediator prepare a mediated settlement agreement for everyone to sign before they leave. From this document, the attorneys draft a decree of divorce which the judge signs after a short presentation by one of the parties and his or her attorney, completing the divorce.

For Most Texans, It's Mandatory

Mediation has changed family law significantly. A process that took years can now be accomplished in months, weeks or even days. Many family courts across the country now advocate mediation in one form or another. One county in Minnesota works with a model called ENE (Early Neutral Evaluation) that guides families through the legal system "quickly, inexpensively and respectfully." Over an 18-month period, nearly 90% of divorcing couples in that county chose to try ENE, and in the majority of those cases that did settle, they were able to resolve all of their issues in one meeting.[12]

Texas has the most progressive and intense use of mediation in the country. Most Texas courts require mediation before they schedule a family law case for trial, and judges operate under varying rules. "Every case in my court that involves child custody goes to mediation," says Judge Lewis. "And the only property cases in which mediation is waived are the ones that can be tried in two hours or less, and those are few and far between."

Beware of Mediation Abusers

Critics of mediation ask how you can mediate with a spouse who is abusive or dishonest. They say you cannot expect someone who is abusing children, hiding assets or having affairs to fully cooperate with the divorce proceeding. Mediation under these circumstances can be very difficult. And the truth is that mediation can be abused by someone who does not negotiate in good faith. That's why you need an attorney as your representative and adviser. Many people who view the mediation process with skepticism still come out with a worthwhile settlement.

Mediation abusers are just one more reason to prepare for a trial, so that if negotiations should fail you're ready for the next step.

Remember the Children

Truth and justice in a divorce case are measured in degrees rather than as absolutes. In other types of civil litigation, the adversarial system may work well. But in those instances, the opposing parties haven't had children together. "Parents don't realize that kids can adapt, but only as well as you let them," says Dr. Ray Levy, child psychologist and author of *Try and Make Me!*, a book for parents and teachers dealing with difficult children. "Once you resolve the situation your kids will move on, but sometimes parents try to make the situation bigger and worse than it really is."

Your children are counting on you to be the adults in this situation. Dragging them through a court battle, rather than settling things quickly and quietly, keeps your children from adjusting to their new life. And while it may satisfy a need for revenge, it may not teach your children the kind of lessons you want them to learn. Once the divorce is over, you'll no longer be married, but you'll still be a parent who needs to cooperate with your children's other parent. Mediation gives you and your spouse a chance to reach an acceptable compromise, which benefits your children. As much as possible, everyone wins in this instance.

The Kitchen Table Deal

An agreement reached between the spouses through direct negotiation is an informal alternative to mediation. Sometimes referred to as a kitchen table deal, this process involves you and your spouse engaging in one or more informal settlement conferences with or without your attorneys. From these conferences you can enter into a binding settlement agreement. To be binding, the agreement must be in writing and state in type that is bold, capitalized or underlined that it is not subject to revocation. You and your spouse will then sign the agreement. If your attorneys are present when you sign the agreement, they must also sign it. If the agreement meets these requirements, it is considered binding on both of you. The court will then review the document. If it finds that the terms are just and right, they will incorporate the terms into the final decree. If not, the court may request that you revise the agreement or set the case for trial.

The provisions of the Texas Family Code that cover binding informal agreements are still a work in progress and are subject to revision. You should check with an attorney before signing anything or attempting to prepare an agreement that is binding, especially if it involves children.

11

Who's at Fault?

PEOPLE SEEKING DIVORCE in Texas don't have to prove improper conduct or other fault grounds for dissolution of a marriage. Since 1969, when the legislature adopted Title 1 of the Texas Family Code, this state has sanctioned no-fault divorce. This does not mean, though, that the cause of the divorce isn't considered.

No-fault divorce was created for people like Lewis. During his divorce in the early 1960s, one party had to accuse the other of awful conduct just to have the divorce granted. The atmosphere in the court was different then. Lewis thought the whole process was cruel. Having to explain and embellish the things his wife had done just to dissolve the marriage seemed unnecessary. Since that day, he and his first wife have not spoken to each other. She still considers him her sworn enemy, and even though he did not intend for that to happen, he feels the system forced him into that position.

The Role of Fault in a No-Fault State

Judges would rather not deal with the issue of fault in a marriage. With all of the complications involved in dividing property and awarding custody of children, though, they often get called upon to make moral judgments about who did what to whom and how that affects the outcome of the divorce. So in reality, fault still matters.

If there is no fault present and the parties merely grow apart, the court still has to consider various factors, such as differences in earning power, when dividing the community assets and debts of a marriage.

Because Texas is a community property state, the court presumes that all property acquired during the marriage is community property and subject to division. However, the Texas Family Code does not mandate an equal division of that property. Instead, the law in Texas calls for a "just and right" division.

The separate property of a spouse generally consists of property owned before marriage, proceeds from the sale of separate property, personal injury awards and gifts or inheritances received either before or during the marriage. Separate property is not divisible by the court, but the one who alleges separate property ownership must prove it with clear and convincing evidence.

If you cannot agree on the division of property, the judge will determine what kind of division is fair and equitable. Those facts might include the length of your marriage, each person's earning potential after the divorce, the types of assets and debts in question and who gets custody of the children. In some cases, who's at fault in the divorce — along with the type of fault — may be a deciding factor.

Types of Fault

Claiming that your spouse was at fault does not include things like snoring too loudly, constantly nagging, or insulting your family. These things might mean that your spouse does not meet your expectations, but they aren't what a trial judge would consider as fault in a divorce.

Q&A

How will the judge punish my spouse for being unfaithful?

"Adultery most likely will not affect visitation time the adulterer is granted with the children, unless there was some inappropriate contact between the paramour and the children or the adultery adversely affected the kids. With property division, though, it's in the court's discretion to award a disproportionate share to the victimized spouse. However, testimony regarding adultery usually involves a very fact-intensive inquiry that may result in facts weighing against BOTH spouses for different reasons, and these can cancel each other out in the judge's mind."

Aubrey Connatser
Family Law Attorney

Examples of fault include:
- Adultery
- Physical abuse of a spouse or child
- Mental abuse of a spouse or child
- Sexual abuse of a spouse or child
- Abandonment for at least one year
- Felony convictions coupled with imprisonment for at least one year

Disproportionate Division of Property

In addition to the fault grounds listed above, there are many other factors a judge can consider that would lead to a disproportionate division of community assets. Those grounds include:

- Addiction to illegal drugs or prescription medicines
- Alcoholism
- Overly suspicious or obsessive behavior
- Excessive gambling or spending
- Mental illness or psychological problems
- Unusual sexual practices
- Benefits the innocent spouse might have derived from continuation of the marriage
- Disparity of earning power of the spouses and their ability to support themselves
- Business opportunities, capacities and abilities of the spouses
- Education and future employability of the spouses
- Health of each spouse
- Age of each spouse
- Needs of the children
- Debts and liabilities
- Tax consequences of the division of property
- Nature of the property involved in the division

- Wasting of community assets by either spouse
- Giving credit for temporary support paid by one spouse to the other
- Community funds used to purchase out-of-state property
- Gifts to or by a spouse during the marriage
- Increase in value of separate property through community efforts by time, talent, labor and effort
- Excessive community property gifts to the children
- Expected inheritance of a spouse
- Attorney's fees to be paid
- Size and nature of the separate estates of each spouse
- Creation of community property through the use of one spouse's separate estate
- Creation of community property by the efforts or lack thereof of each spouse
- Fraud on the community estate
- Actual fraud committed by one spouse
- Constructive fraud committed by one spouse

Can You Prove It?

If you feel your spouse displays any of the behaviors that constitute fault or support a disproportionate division of property in your favor, ask yourself if you can prove it to the satisfaction of a judge or jury. Opinion, speculation and rumor are not admissible as evidence in court, and attorneys are good at cleaning up their client's act for court appearances. How many times have you seen an evil-looking mug shot of a defendant only to later see news footage of someone in the courtroom who looks like an investment banker. You cannot expect the court to see your spouse as guilty of fault based only on your word. You must be able to prove whatever you allege. That proof can be witnesses — yourself or others. It can be a paper trail including receipts and bank withdrawals. It can even be photographs, video or audio recordings. Whatever form it takes, you must have proof. Otherwise you could come out looking like a vindictive spouse.

The courts consider all of the evidence and decide if it demonstrates the behavior of a reasonably prudent married person who is properly attending to family duties. People in successful marriages are rarely seen in bars late at night in the company of a person of the opposite sex. They are not at that person's apartment several times each week. And they don't make hundreds of cellphone calls to the person late at night. In this type of situation, good divorce lawyers put the burden of explaining the circumstances on the spouse who has been accused.

Your judge will probably have a keen sense of what actions are reasonable in a marriage. If you are guilty of marital misconduct, you need to consider how your actions will look. You and your lawyer can decide how to handle these issues. If you are not guilty of what your spouse alleges, you and your lawyer must decide how to combat the misconceptions.

12

Take Time to Evaluate Your Attorney

AT SOME POINT DURING YOUR DIVORCE, you'll probably ask yourself if you are getting your money's worth from your attorney. Usually this happens after the initial rush to gather information, after the first settlement discussions and after depositions and other discovery are complete. When you reach this point, you're probably on an emotional roller coaster and not thinking as clearly as you normally would. To begin evaluating your attorney's performance, ask yourself the following questions:

- Are you closer to resolving the divorce since hiring your attorney?
- Do you feel that the settlement will be close to what your attorney predicted in the beginning, or have those promises gone out the window?
- Will you and your spouse be able to deal amicably with each other when the case is over?

- How much is the divorce costing you, and can you realistically say that you will emerge from the divorce with more than you paid in attorney's fees?

It is smart to evaluate your attorney, but be realistic in your assessment and understand that lawyers are not magicians and they cannot perform miracles. Take notice of whether your attorney demonstrates knowledge, prepares well and suggests appropriate plans to deal with the issues at hand.

Attorney-Client Mismatch

Different attorneys have different work ethics, communication styles and ideas of how to handle a case. The biggest complaint clients have about their attorneys, and one of the major reasons for grievances being filed against them, is a failure to communicate.

By the time you get into the real work of your case, you'll know a lot about your attorney and whether you work well together. Finding a new attorney at this point can be very disruptive and unsettling. So even if you feel that you and your attorney do not see eye to eye on your case, you may still be able to reach a satisfactory settlement without making a change.

Lack of Communication

Good communication between you and your attorney is essential. Plainly put, your attorney should update you regularly. One woman found a divorce attorney she liked very much. The initial interview and the time leading up to filing the divorce petition went smoothly. Then a couple of months went by without the attorney returning her repeated phone calls. Unable to get a status report on her case, she began to ask for the legal assistant, who referred her back to the attorney. The woman became extremely frustrated that she had to beg for news from someone she was paying.

Eventually, six months passed and still she had no notice that the divorce had been filed. She sent faxes and letters to the attorney, with no response. Finally, she resorted to lying to the receptionist, telling her that she had failed to return the attorney's calls. The receptionist gave her his cellphone number. After several attempts, she managed to get him on the phone. Without skipping a beat, the attorney said that things were finally beginning to happen and that he was actually on his way to the courthouse to deal with a matter regarding her divorce. He told her that he had been meaning to call her because they had received a settlement offer from the other side. When she asked what it was, he replied, "I don't know. I haven't read it."

This is certainly not the type of communication to expect from your attorney.

Too Much Activity

Sometimes you can stir your attorney into too much action, which results in a lot of wasted effort and money. Eventually you may get frustrated and angry at this waste of your resources, not realizing that you caused it the first place.

One man, a physician, shopped around for the meanest lawyer he could find to handle his divorce. When he found one, he paid the man a $25,000 retainer to begin his complex divorce which included children and lots of property. Soon his lawyer had created a flurry of documents, which included the divorce petition and numerous motions full of accusations about the wife, based on information given by the doctor. Whenever the doctor called his attorney's office, the secretary always put him through immediately. He engaged the attorney in long, rambling discussions about strategy and the emotional drama of the divorce. The doctor even called the attorney on evenings and weekends.

With all of this commotion, the initial retainer went quickly and the doctor had to replenish it with another $25,000 and then

$10,000 more. Things were starting to happen though, so he felt it was worth it. Meanwhile, his life was in a complete state of upheaval. He had been close to his in-laws before, but they were now furious with him. And his children were so upset that they needed counseling. The doctor's medical practice also began to suffer as an unusual number of patients canceled appointments. The tension was so great that he began having trouble sleeping.

Finally, he'd had enough. He called the attorney to complain about the expenses and the chaos. The attorney reminded the doctor that his instructions had been to spare no expense, to be aggressive and to keep the pressure on his wife. The doctor replied that he also wanted to win, and that after having spent $60,000 he was farther away from winning than when he started.

This client eventually learned a hard lesson about winning at all cost. He and his attorney sat down and began to handle the case in a much more constructive fashion. Once things calmed down, they quickly reached a settlement.

The moral of this story is that if you set out to make your spouse miserable, you're likely to get more than you bargained for and end up with a lot less money and infinitely more chaos. While it is wise to share your goals with your attorney, keep in mind that your judgment may be clouded by the emotions brought out by your current situation. Do not pay for an attorney's advice if you are not going to heed it.

It is also a good idea, later in the case, to reexamine what you said in your first meeting. People usually think more clearly once they get past some of the emotion. It is the lawyer's responsibility to inform you of what is reasonable, and it is your responsibility to use that information constructively.

Legal Eagle, Fly Away

If it becomes apparent that your lawyer is not making as much progress as you would like, you may have to consider seeking new counsel. This is a drastic move you should make only after asking yourself if you are doing this because you aren't making progress or because this attorney won't comply with your unrealistic demands.

Don't be like the man who smokes three packs of cigarettes a day and continually fires doctors until he finds one who says it's his right to smoke. That doesn't mean it's suddenly okay to smoke. All it means is that when he contracts lung cancer, his doctor will be partially to blame.

It can be expensive, in terms of both money and progress, to constantly change attorneys. And doing so without good reason may indicate that you are the problem and not the other way around. If several lawyers tell you that you cannot achieve your goals under Texas law, you might have to change your frame of mind, not your attorney.

Legal malpractice attorney Randy Johnston hears the laments of divorcing people at his Dallas office all day long, but he takes only the most egregious cases against family lawyers. "The moment I hear that a prospective client has had three or four divorce attorneys, I have to wonder what's wrong with the client. Even if that person has a justifiable case, I just get the feeling that we're in for a whole lot of trouble."

So you should engage in a little self-evaluation when problems arise with your lawyer. If you decide that finding a new attorney is the best course of action, the process is fairly easy. Simply call your lawyer and ask to have your file sent to you or to the new attorney you have retained. If you cannot reach your attorney by phone, send a fax or letter and call the office to confirm that it was received. For the good of your case, the timing of the change is important. If you make a change just prior to a court appearance, you can hurt your case and cause your new attorney to begin the representation well behind the opposition.

Whenever you terminate an attorney, ask for a refund of any unused portion of your retainer or pay any existing balance due, subject to the terms of your written fee agreement.

The bottom line is that this is your divorce, and you are entitled to be represented by legal counsel you respect. You need someone you can communicate with, one whose representation will allow you to sleep at night.

In a Market of Bulls and Bears, This Is Some Dog

"In one case I mediated, the husband and wife both worked and had a fairly substantial community estate. However, they seemed far more interested in who got ownership of Diablo, their dog. Each one insisted that settlement was impossible without him. I told them that we would first divide the property and then we would conduct an auction for Diablo.

"Part of the property settlement included an $11,000 tax refund. When the bidding began, the wife offered to give up her half of the tax refund ($5,500) in exchange for the dog. The husband rejected the bid and offered his share of the refund plus an additional $5,000, making the bid a total of $10,500. The wife raised the bid another $5,000. Unable to resist, the husband took the $15,500, fell out of love with the dog, and the wife waltzed away with her valuable pooch. Both parties were very happy."

Harry Tindall
Family Law Attorney

Part Three: Decisions Involving Children and Assets

13

Custody of the Children

PARENTS ARGUE OVER CUSTODY of their children for many reasons. Sometimes they are motivated by pride or revenge, and now and then a parent will file for custody simply to gain a bargaining chip in negotiations over marital assets. But most of the time, parents believe they are acting in the best interests of their children. When you cannot come to an agreement on your own, a judge or jury will decide for you. Keep in mind that decisions are based on the facts and circumstances surrounding the breakup of your marriage, and these things don't always give people the whole picture.

When Don filed for divorce, he never intended to ask for custody of the children. His wife was a stay-at-home mom, so she was their primary caregiver and the one who took them to the doctor and their other activities. Although he coached his son's baseball team, Don was a traditional guy who filled the role of family provider and assumed he would remain in that role after the divorce. He was content to play second chair in the raising of his kids.

As divorce proceedings began, Don discovered that he had to referee arguments between his wife and daughter more frequently.

It was only after the tension between him and his wife reached epic proportions — when he moved out of their Amarillo home — that he decided he couldn't just give up his children and would need to reevaluate his relationship with them. His wife was increasingly stressed and high-strung, so the children went to him when they really needed to talk. As time passed, friends told him how distant his wife was with the children.

Don decided he could not just walk away. He knew he had a slim chance to gain sole custody of his children, but when they were older he at least wanted them to know he tried. His lawyer recommended joint custody, which is the preferred choice in this state, and they began to work in that direction.

This is just one example of what might happen as you go through your divorce and begin to fully understand the impact it will have on the daily lives of your children. Each child custody arrangement is unique and complex. According to family court Judge Marilea Lewis, "Even if you cannot come to a full agreement regarding the children, resolve any matters you can ahead of time and present them to the court. Child custody is an emotionally wrenching issue and it's difficult to weed through it all in the course of litigation."

In high-conflict cases, you can request a parenting coordinator to help resolve your parenting issues, and in cases where the judge deems it necessary, the court will appoint one for you on its own. Parenting coordinators do not make decisions for you, but they can help you reach agreements that can be presented to the court. They can also help both sides comply with the court's orders.

The History of Custody

Child custody in Texas is like a pendulum swinging radically one way and then the other. In the mid-19th century, children were considered the father's property, along with almost everything else the couple owned. And since the man had all the assets, it was not conceivable that the woman could take care of the children. Therefore, in those rare instances of divorce, the father usually assumed custody of the kids.

In the early 20th century, women won the right to vote along with a steady increase in an overall level of their rights. No longer were they the property of their husbands. As the number of divorces increased, women gained a special status in relation to their children and were automatically awarded custody unless the father could prove the woman was an unfit mother.

This standard continued until the late 1970s, especially in cases involving young children. Today, the pendulum has swung back toward the middle. Men are gaining custody with increasing frequency, mainly due to changes in society and the way we live. Many households now have two wage earners, and couples share childcare responsibilities more evenly than in the past. Judges are now more open to seeing men as primary caregivers. In fact, the Texas Family Code now instructs both judges and juries who are awarding custody not to give any preference to either party solely on the basis of gender. In Texas, you can request à jury in a custody trial, and men who want custody sometimes use this option if their attorney thinks they'll have a better chance of pleading their case to a group of peers instead of to the judge assigned to the case.

Types of Custody

Whether you agree on custody during settlement negotiations or the court awards it, there are two types of custody in Texas: sole and joint. Your rights under the different custody arrangements can vary greatly.

If you are awarded sole custody, the children live with you and you have the right and responsibility to make all major decisions relating to them. This includes establishing their primary residence and making all medical, educational and social decisions. Your former spouse usually has visitation rights, which might include weekly visits plus certain holidays and a month each summer.

Q&A

Does joint custody mean he gets the children half the time?

"That's a popular misconception, but the short answer would be no. Joint managing conservatorship only relates to the rights and powers divided between parents. Either the two parties decide the amount of possession or a judge decides it for them."

Karen Turner
Family Law Attorney

If the court awards joint custody, it will usually designate one of you as the primary custodian, even though you may share parental rights and duties. Typically, the children live with the primary custodian for the majority of the time and spend time with the other parent according to a specified schedule. Joint custody arrangements must also specify which decisions each parent controls. One benefit of joint custody is that it tends to encourage parents to cooperate.

Texas Law Favors Joint Custody

Joint custody has been a part of Texas family law for years, but at one time it was only considered suitable for parents who could settle disputes involving their children in a civilized manner. Consequently, the courts only awarded it when both parties asked for it.

In 1987, the Texas Legislature amended the family code to allow judges and juries to consider joint custody in all cases, even when there was no agreement between the parents. Now the courts can force parents who cannot stand the sight of each other to work out their differences for the sake of their children. This provision allows both parents to retain some control over their children's lives and alleviates the stigma parents feel when they give up custody or have it taken away by the courts.

The label of joint custody is sometimes misunderstood. Just because you have joint custody does not mean you and your spouse each retain a 50/50 vote in the decisions concerning your children. A judge can determine each aspect of the arrangement or you and you spouse can negotiate it yourselves. Over the past several years, the Texas Legislature has modified the family code so that each of the parental rights and duties can be allocated in one of three ways:

- Independently (Each parent has equal authority and can act on their own.)

- Jointly (The parents must agree or go back to court.)
- Exclusively (One parent has all the authority.)

Recognizing that parents don't always agree when making joint decisions, it is a common practice to include a tie-breaking mechanism such as the opinion of a school counselor or a mental health expert. Settlement agreements sometimes give a right to one parent exclusively, on the condition that the other parent is consulted. But this condition is nearly impossible to enforce because it is difficult to determine what satisfies the consultation requirement.

In all joint custody orders, the court must specify which parent determines the children's legal residence and whether the residence is restricted to a particular geographic area. For example, the court may designate a particular county and all neighboring counties, one or more school districts or an entire state.

The courts recognize that if the primary parent moves the child to another state, it inhibits a close relationship with the other parent. Relocations are considered on a case-by-case basis, and generally the primary parent must provide a compelling reason for moving the child away from the other parent.

Even if you have a joint custody arrangement, child support payments will probably be awarded because support is based on the income of the non-primary parent and, to some extent, the needs of the children.

Joint custody does not fit every situation, but if two good parents are involved, it is often the best way for both of you to maintain close relationships with your children. Appendix B of this book is an example of the language in a typical joint custody order.

When Is Sole Custody Appropriate?

Although Texas courts favor joint custody, there are circumstances where sole custody is the only real option. This may occur when:

- One parent completely abandons the family
- One parent is unwilling to share responsibility for the children or cooperate in decision making on their behalf
- One parent is unable to participate in decision making due to some form of incapacity
- It has been proven that one parent harmed the children and/or the other parent either physically, emotionally or sexually
- Animosity between the two parents is so great that forcing them to cooperate could be detrimental to the children.

Who Should Be the Primary Custodian?

In a custody dispute, the court wants to know which parent has been the primary caregiver of the children during the marriage. This parent normally receives primary custody, unless there are significant conflicting circumstances or problems with that parent to prevent it. The parent who does most of the following generally has an advantage when determining who will be the children's primary caregiver:

- Who helps them get dressed for school?
- Who fixes their breakfast?
- Who packs their lunch for school?
- Who helps them with homework?
- Who participates in their school activities?
- Who takes care of them after school?
- Who bathes them?
- Who takes them to the doctor?
- Who takes them shopping?
- Who takes them to religious activities?
- Who arranges for their extracurricular activities?
- Who helps them in various stages of development?
- Who nurtures them?

It is also important for the judge or jury to know about changes that will take place in your household after the divorce. For instance, a stay-at-home mom might need to begin working outside the home, grandparents might take over some childcare duties or a father might forego a business opportunity to become more involved in everyday activities.

Your parenting abilities may change significantly because of your divorce, and the court considers all of this in the custody arrangement.

What You Should Know About Your Children Before a Custody Fight

If you have participated in the majority of the activities listed in the previous section, you should know the answers to the following questions. Give yourself this quiz to see how much you really know about your children:

- Who is their doctor?
- Where is the doctor's office?
- What allergies do they have?
- Who is their dentist?
- What is the name of their school principal?
- What is their teacher's name?
- What is their favorite subject in school?
- Who is their day care provider?
- How often do they go to day care?
- Name their three best friends.
- What is their favorite book?
- What is their favorite color?
- What special needs do they have?
- What size shoes do they wear?
- What clothing sizes do they wear?

Children are rarely put on the stand, but that does not mean judges and juries rely solely on the word of the parents. "In many cases, someone with experience interviews the children and talks with them about their activities, their schedules and who takes them places," says Judge Lewis. "In Dallas, we have Family Court Services. Their social workers are trained to interview children and give the court guidance on who the primary caregiver has been."

Sometimes a parent means well but hasn't taken an active role in childcare. If this is the case with you, time is necessary to establish a stronger role in your children's lives and learn more about them before asking for custody.

One man questioned his wife's ability to care for their children. Although he worked long hours and traveled for his company, he knew that would change after the divorce. For several months, he worked at strengthening his relationship with his children. After a particularly disturbing weekend at home, when the mother repeatedly became violent with the kids, he alerted his attorney to file the divorce and sent the children to stay with a relative until the dust settled. Even though he wasn't the primary caregiver during the marriage, he prepared well and could show how his wife's mental state affected his kids. He won sole custody and she received a safe amount of visitation time.

Custody/Visitation Problems

Young children are most likely to become entangled in their parents' problems. If you have young children, you can almost guarantee that visitation will become a problem at some point in the future. No settlement agreement can address all the potential circumstances you will encounter as you raise children from infancy to adolescence. Disputes between parents, stepparents and significant others can arise from even the simplest issues, such as being late to pick up or drop off the children. One parent will sometimes call his or her attorney because the ex returned the children

10 minutes late. This may seem extreme, but divorced parents frequently magnify minor annoyances and aggravations, sometimes beyond all reason. Often married people run late with the same frequency as divorced people. Yet when you have a court order spelling out a defined visitation schedule, some people choose to see lateness as an intentional manipulation of the rules so carefully set out by the court.

"Parents frequently try to control things they had no control over when they were married," says child psychologist Dr. Ray Levy. "It's unclear why they think they can control it after a divorce."

Being late is usually the result of bad time management or getting caught in traffic, but it's often construed as a form of rebellion when a parent is unhappy with the current arrangement. Unfortunately, the children get caught in the middle. "When handing the kids off, act like business partners," says Dr. Levy. "Be on time and be civil. And if you have a key to your ex's house for pickups and drop-offs, respect your ex's privacy. Don't snoop around and get into his or her personal life."

When visitation becomes a tool for revenge, the children suffer because they often are denied time with the other parent. This was true in the case of the mother who told her child, "I would like to let you go to the game, but I can't trust your father to bring you home on time." There was the father who said, "You can't go to your mother's because she always lets you stay up way past your bedtime and you have a big game tomorrow." These bitter declarations speak volumes about the visitation problems these families will have in the future.

Standard Visitation and Access

Disputes over access to children are a common problem couples have after they divorce. Since many parents have trouble determining a schedule on their own, the court applies the standard possession order in most cases. The standard possession order outlines when your children will be with you and when they will be with your ex. The order is used to ensure that children maintain a relationship with each of you after the divorce.

The court aims to create balance for the children. To some extent, a judge will consider their needs over the needs of the parents. You may establish your own schedule during settlement negotiations that grants more or less than the standard visitation. But a judge will seldom limit a parent's access to less than the standard possession order unless you prove that this extra visitation will somehow harm your children.

The standard visitation schedules are based on distance. If you and your ex live less than 100 miles apart, you will share shorter, more frequent blocks of time with the children. If you live more than 100 miles apart, a different standard schedule accounts for travel time and expenses. You can find a copy of the standard possession order at Appendix C (page 262) of this book. Consult your attorney to find out how it applies to your case.

Once you have a set visitation schedule, you must comply with it unless both you and your ex agree to changes. This agreement is not a suggestion; it is a court order. One mother told her children so many bad things about their father that they did not want to go with him for their scheduled visits. She believed he lied to them, so she gave the children a tape recorder and told them to record all of their conversations with their father. Whenever he called or came to the door, they did as requested and secretly turned on the recorder. The mother said she could not understand why they would not go with him. Eventually, the father discovered the source of the problem.

When he later sued for custody, the children testified that they loved him very much and had only refused to go with him because they did not want to hurt their mother's feelings. The woman not only taught her children to lie, but she also created a barrier that nearly destroyed their relationship with their father. The court found her in contempt for willfully violating the visitation order.

Small children are rarely called to give testimony on the witness stand. Judges and juries view this strategy harshly, so you and your attorney must have a good reason for calling a child to testify. Lawyers who put a child on the stand merely to ask which parent he or she wants to live with take a huge risk with the court and also can damage the well-being of the child.

Sharing Your Children

Though your children are an essential part of your family, they did not cause this divorce and they are entitled to have two parents who continue to treat them with love and respect. Unless there is an abusive situation, they should have large amounts of quality time with each of you. You will have differences of opinion over who is the better parent, but keep these disputes between the two of you. Too many parents use the children as pawns against each other.

"The greatest gift you can give your children is permission to love the other parent," says Dr. Maryanne Watson. "When you do this, they will love you even more in return." It is common and even natural to feel angry toward your spouse, but it is cruel and damaging to put your children in the middle.

"If you have to bite your tongue until it bleeds, do not say negative things about your ex in front of your children," says Dr. Watson. "Because if you do, they will become defensive and feel hurt on behalf of the other parent. When children grow up and become adults, they often gravitate toward the parent who was maligned."

One woman refrained from talking badly about the children's father but continually criticized his new wife, their stepmother. The children were less enthusiastic about visiting their father and his seemingly poor choice degraded him in their eyes. When the children grew up, though, their view began to change. By the time they were in their late twenties, the children looked forward to conversations and visits with their father, but their mother complained that she rarely heard from them and had to pressure them to visit her.

How much harm your children suffer from the divorce depends largely on how you handle it. They will always remember this period in their lives, and if you neglect them or use them as pawns they will never forget it. One day the games you played with their lives will become more apparent and no amount of apologizing will change it.

Parenting Classes

Many family court judges have a policy of requiring both parents to complete parenting classes in all contested cases involving children. Other judges order these classes for litigants on a case-by-case basis.

These are not the very general type of group therapy sessions where parents discuss their feelings about divorce. Rather, these are serious classes focused on educating parents about how divorce affects children and teaches them techniques for parenting during and after the divorce.

The resources section at Appendix F (page 279) in the back of this book lists some of the programs that offer parenting classes commonly ordered by the courts.

Q&A

*How much child support
will I pay (or receive)?*

"Child support is most often determined by using the state mandated guidelines, which calculate child support as certain percentages of net income, with that net income capped at $7,500. For instance, child support for one child would be 20% of net monthly income or as much as $1,500 per month. For two children, it is 25% of net monthly income or as much as $1,875 and so on. Child support can exceed the guideline amounts in cases where there are unusual needs or circumstances."

*Kevin Fuller
Family Law Attorney*

14

Child Support

IN TEXAS, CHILD SUPPORT IS CALCULATED by using the guidelines contained in the Texas Family Code. The charts that accompany the guidelines are updated regularly. Under the family code, the court may order either or both parents to support a child until one of the following occurs:

- The child reaches the age of 18 or graduates from high school (whichever happens later)
- The child marries or has his or her minority removed by law
- The child dies

Under the court order, the parent who pays child support is called the obligor, while the parent who receives the support is the obligee. The formula to calculate child support uses the obligor's net monthly resources, which consist of monthly gross wages and other income (rental income, dividends, etc.) minus taxes, union dues and the cost of health insurance for the children. Only the resources of the obligor are considered unless the child has special needs which exceed the guideline support amount. If the obligor has remarried, the resources of the new spouse are *not* included in the formula.

Calculating Child Support

The amount of the child support payments you will pay or receive depends on the number of children you have and the obligor's net monthly resources (which consist of monthly gross wages and other income minus taxes, union dues and the cost of health insurance for the children). The amount for the first child is 20% of the obligor's net monthly resources. The increases are currently five percent per child as follows:

1 child	20% of obligor's net resources
2 children	25% of obligor's net resources
3 children	30% of obligor's net resources
4 children	35% of obligor's net resources
5 children	40% of obligor's net resources
6+ children	Not less than the amount for 5 children[13]

Take a look at the following example. A man earns $4,800 per month in gross wages and has no other income. After taxes, union dues and children's health insurance expenses, his net monthly income is $3,920. Because he has two children, his child support payments are 25% of his net income, or $980 per month. Note that the percentages are slightly reduced if he also supports children from another relationship.

Normally, the obligor must not only provide the children with health insurance but also pay a percentage of the children's medical expenses which are not covered by insurance. The obligor can provide insurance through an employer, a separate policy or even by paying for the children's policy through the obligee's employment. If the obligor neglects to provide insurance as ordered, he or

Q&A

If my ex fails to pay his child support, can I keep him from seeing the children?

"Absolutely not! If you fail to follow the court order concerning visitation, you can be jailed for contempt. Access to the children is separate and apart from the issue of child support. If he doesn't pay child support, you need to file a motion for enforcement. The good news for the parent entitled to receive child support is that courts throughout the state consider child support a top priority."

Julie Crawford
Family Law Attorney

she must pay all of the children's medical expenses, regardless of whether insurance would have covered them.

If the obligor is self-employed, it may be difficult, if not impossible, to estimate his or her income. Some self-employed people receive payments in cash, income that is difficult to prove without cooperation. If your spouse is self-employed, income tax returns, financial statements, bank records and other documentation are extremely important in proving your case for child support. Sometimes an attorney will use spending habits to show the court that the obligor's income is higher than has been stated.

Special Circumstances

The court cannot exceed guidelines based solely on the parents' abilities to pay. If your children have disabilities, health problems or special educational needs which exceed the guideline amount, the court may follow different rules when deciding the amount of support in your case. The court initially caps the obligor's net monthly resources at $7,500 when calculating the amount of child support. Then, if the children's financial needs exceed the support payments calculated from that amount, both parents' income and assets are evaluated to determine if the obligor will pay additional child support.

If you and your spouse plan to share equal time with the children, the court may not apply the usual child support guidelines. Additionally, any special or extraordinary needs of the children can justify a deviation from the guidelines. Often an offset amount based on the difference in the parents' incomes is ordered in these cases.

Child Support Collection

Child support is one of the most overlooked and underpaid debts in our society. The federal government estimates that if all child support was paid, there would be almost no children living in poverty in this country. Across the nation, obligor parents owed more than $111 billion in child support in 2005. Texas alone accounted for more than $8.9 billion of that figure, representing more than a million children.[14]

Even though problems exist in child support collection, the Texas Family Code says that child support payments and visitation are separate issues. You cannot deny visitation if child support is unpaid, and conversely you cannot withhold child support if visitation is denied. Parents frequently use these tactics against each other, either withholding money or visitation from the other parent. By doing so, you can be found in contempt of court and earn fines and jail time. In addition, statistics clearly show that when the parent without primary custody sees the children regularly, he or she is more likely to pay child support and help with other related expenses.

The Texas Attorney General's office oversees child support collections. You can find a local office of the attorney general in the government listings of your phone book or by checking their website online. Several private companies exist that will collect child support in exchange for a percentage of the money they recover. If you use one of these companies, here's a warning: do not pay any fees in advance. Check your Yellow Pages directory under "Child Support Collections" for a list of local companies.

The family code also provides for the State Disbursement Unit in San Antonio to receive court-ordered child support payments and forward them to obligee parents. If you need a record of child support payments for a court hearing about unpaid support, the State Disbursement Unit can provide one.

Support for College

Unlike some other states, the courts in Texas cannot require a parent to pay for college expenses and tuition after a child reaches the age of majority at 18 years old. So if you want these expenses included in your decree of divorce, you and your spouse will have to outline this in a settlement agreement. College expenses may include tuition, books and room and board. You can also specify other items such as a weekly allowance, fees, computer equipment, fraternity and sorority expenses and transportation costs. Since this agreement is not decided in court, you are free to specify that one parent pay all of these expenses or you may split the costs any way you can agree.

List the anticipated expenses in the settlement agreement to avoid any confusion in the future. If your child earns scholarships, you normally credit their value against the expected payments. Regardless of your agreement to pay for college expenses, child support payments and orders for payment of the child's medical insurance and expenses do not continue after the child reaches 18 years of age and graduates from high school, unless you also make that part of your settlement agreement.

Q&A

Are you entitled to alimony in Texas?

"Even if your spouse made $10 million a year, he or she would pay no more than $2,500 per month in alimony. Except under special circumstances, the alimony statute is for spouses who were married for at least 10 years, lack any substantial assets and are unable to earn enough money to cover basic living expenses. The maximum amount of alimony you can receive is 20% of your ex-spouse's gross income, up to a maximum payment of $2,500 per month for no more than three years in almost all circumstances."

Kevin Fuller
Family Law Attorney

15

Alimony and Maintenance

ALIMONY DOES EXIST IN TEXAS, but the narrow guidelines prevent most people from qualifying for it. If you expect to receive alimony as your main form of income after the divorce, consult with your attorney. Unless you can negotiate it as part of a settlement agreement, you may need to start making other plans.

The Alimony Statute

The Texas Legislature passed an alimony statute in 1995. They intended it to provide temporary support for a divorced spouse (usually the wife) who lacks the job skills and assets needed to support herself and her children as a result of being a stay-at-home parent for many years. In these cases, alimony provides income to live on while the woman goes back to school or in some other way gains the skills needed to support herself. This training should increase her earning capacity so that she no longer needs alimony.

If you qualify to receive alimony under the guidelines listed below, the court can order that you receive up to 20% of your spouse's gross income or $2,500 per month, whichever is less, for up to three years. Keep in mind that these are the basic guidelines under the Texas Family Code. Consult with your attorney for the exact legal wording and qualifications to see if they apply to your situation.

You are eligible for court-ordered maintenance (alimony) only if you meet one of the following two conditions:

1. Married for 10 years or longer and lack sufficient assets (including assets awarded to you in the divorce) to provide for your minimum reasonable needs, and
    - Cannot work because of a physical or mental disability;
    - Cannot work outside the home because you take care of a child with a disability, or
    - Clearly lack the skills needed to earn enough money to provide for your minimum reasonable needs.
2. Your spouse was convicted of or received deferred adjudication for a crime that constitutes family violence within the two years before the divorce was filed or while the divorce was pending.

The Alimony Reality

The problem with the Texas version of alimony is that most people who think they need it don't qualify for it and most people who qualify will never see the money. If you have any substantial assets, or receive them in the divorce, you won't qualify for alimony. If your marital assets are limited enough that you do qualify, your spouse probably doesn't earn enough to pay it. And even if the court orders alimony, it can be modified or eliminated by court order after the divorce is over.

Poor women probably qualify for alimony more than any other socioeconomic group in Texas, but the majority of people who actually receive alimony are in the middle- and high-income brackets who agree to accept alimony payments rather than their full portion of the community assets at the time of divorce.

People prefer to make alimony payments for several reasons. There are tax advantages to making payments, and if the spouse receiving the payments also takes care of the children, payments give some assurance that funds will be available for the children's ongoing expenses. When a couple's only marital asset is a business or a home, they may agree to alimony instead of selling the business or home to divide the equity.

Under the Texas Family Code, the courts presume that spouses deserve alimony only if they actively seek suitable employment or develop the skills needed to find a good job during the separation period and pending divorce. One exception to this rule is when a spouse is disabled or has to stay home to care for a disabled child.

How the Court Decides

When the court awards alimony, it considers the following factors in determining the nature, amount, duration and manner of the payments:

- Financial resources of the receiving spouse
- Education and employment skills of both spouses
- Length of the marriage
- Age, employment history, earning ability and physical and emotional condition of the receiving spouse
- Financial ability of the paying spouse
- Any financial mismanagement or concealment by either spouse
- The comparative financial resources of the spouses, including medical, retirement, insurance or other benefits
- Contributions to education, training or increased earning power by one spouse to the other

- Property brought to the marriage by either spouse
- Contribution of a spouse as homemaker
- Any marital misconduct by the spouse who would receive alimony
- Efforts by the receiving spouse to pursue employment counseling

Temporary Spousal Support

Temporary spousal support is much more common than alimony in Texas. The difference between the two is that the first covers the period while the divorce is pending and the second goes into effect only after the divorce is final. Temporary spousal support eases the transition from one household to another and preserves the lifestyle of each spouse as much as possible with the disposable income they share. The spouse with the least resources normally receives temporary spousal support, especially if that spouse has temporary custody of the children and the child support coupled with their own income will not cover their expenses while the divorce is pending.

16

Insurance and Taxes

YOU MAY NOT DWELL ON INSURANCE AND TAXES when you think of making decisions in your divorce, but they will affect your future income and expenses. In your negotiations, address the topics of health insurance, life insurance, tax refunds and taxes owed, including both income and property taxes. It's also important to know that you cannot file a joint federal income tax return for the year in which your divorce becomes final.

Often one spouse handles more of the financial matters in the relationship, which puts the other spouse at a disadvantage when it comes time to make financial decisions during a divorce. This was the case with David and Lauren. David accommodated Lauren's every request in their negotiations. But he was not known for his generosity, so Lauren suspected he had ulterior motives. Each time they discussed something she wanted, he said he wanted her to have it. Lauren reviewed all the paperwork on their assets, hoping to find the reason for his kindness, but it remained hidden for nearly a year. David was an accountant who always prepared their income tax returns, and he knew something Lauren didn't. The IRS owed them a large refund from the last year of their marriage, and because of the wording of their agreement he put the entire refund in his own pocket.

To avoid getting caught in situations like this, consult with an accountant about the tax consequences related to your divorce and with a financial planner or other expert about your insurance needs. Your attorney can refer you to someone if you don't know any professionals in these areas.

Tax Liabilities and Refunds

Consider any previous and future income tax liabilities and refunds in your settlement agreement. Your attorney should add language that specifies who is responsible if you find out after the divorce that you owe additional taxes and penalties, especially in case of an audit. "The settlement agreement needs specific and careful wording regarding income taxes," says Jim Wingate, CPA and family law attorney. "Taxes are a complex subject. You can't just state that each spouse pays or receives half. You have to spell out everything."

Vague wording was at issue in one case where the husband and wife each agreed to pay half of the income taxes owed for the last year of their marriage. When the taxes were prepared, the couple's total tax liability was $20,000, but they only owed $5,000 because the wife's employer had withheld $12,000 and the husband, who was self-employed, had paid in $3,000. The wife argued that she had already paid her half of the total tax liability and then some. In fact, she argued that the husband owed her $2,000. The husband did not agree, claiming that the wife owed $2,500, half of the amount due. He finally gave in and paid the $5,000. Afterwards, the wife filed a motion to recover the additional $2,000.

When a spouse signs a joint income tax return without knowing what it contains, an audit or deficiency in payment can take that person by surprise after the divorce. In the past, the IRS required spouses to pay for tax liabilities caused by their exes, even if they knew nothing about the deficiency. In 1998, IRS reforms exempted certain spouses from payment of tax bills due to the actions of an ex-spouse. Your attorney or accountant can advise you on these matters.

Determining which one of you receives the income tax exemptions for the children is another important element of your settlement agreement. Generally, the primary custodial parent claims the exemptions unless you agree to alternate, split the exemptions (with more than one child) or for the other parent to claim them. Have a tax professional evaluate your options and the effect they will have on you.

If one of you has very little income, claiming the exemptions probably won't help. Instead, the exemptions may have a greater benefit for the spouse who earns the majority of the income. This spouse may be willing to increase child support payments in exchange for the right to claim the exemption. Your attorney can help you incorporate the effect of this benefit into your overall settlement. There is a level of income, though, where the higher wage earner loses the benefit of any exemption for the children under the Internal Revenue Code.

For a noncustodial parent to claim the exemption, the custodial parent must fill out IRS form 8332, Release of Claim to Exemption for Child of Divorced or Separated Parents. A copy of this form is located at Appendix E (page 278) or you can print a copy from the website at www.IRS.gov. The form must be attached to the noncustodial parent's tax return. You can specify that the release is for only the current year or for future years as well, although the IRS recommends, "To help ensure future support [payments], you may not want to release your claim to the child's exemption for future years."

The agreement to execute this release each year can be conditioned on the timely payment of child support and on the obligor not seeking a reduction in support payments. Consult with your lawyer and accountant concerning these issues to protect your interests.

Property taxes should also be considered. If you are to receive real estate or proceeds from the sale of real estate in the divorce, you should check with your local appraisal district to find out if any taxes are owed on the property and what taxes will be due for the current year. You may want your spouse to take responsibility for a prorated portion of the taxes due for the year the divorce becomes final. If your spouse is to receive the real estate, the documents should make clear whether he or she will pay the taxes.

Health Insurance for the Children

The parent who pays child support normally provides health insurance for any minor children until they reach majority and graduate from high school. If a child attends college, you can agree for either parent to continue coverage until the child graduates or reaches a certain age, usually 23 years old. In most cases, health insurance is available through an employer of one of the parents. If not, usually the parent who pays child support must obtain individual health insurance to cover the children. Keep in mind that the obligor parent must reimburse the obligee parent for any premiums paid if the health insurance is through the obligee's employer.

Most often, spouses share the responsibility for their children's medical expenses not covered by health insurance. The decree usually states that each parent must pay a certain percentage of any uninsured medical expenses, including deductibles, copays and reasonable charges for doctor, hospital, medical, prescription drug, optical, dental, orthodontic and other medically related expenses. Do not take this issue lightly because most major medical expenses are unplanned. If disaster strikes, the costs can be astronomical. For instance, if a child is diagnosed with a major illness, such as leukemia, the expenses can be devastating and could lead to one or both parents declaring bankruptcy.

Health Insurance for the Spouse

Health insurance for you or your spouse can become a major issue in your case if you both currently have health insurance through one of your employers. One of you will need to find new insurance, because few insurance plans will provide coverage for an ex-spouse after a certain period to time. If you need new insurance, you have several options. Obtaining coverage through your employer is generally the easiest and least expensive solution.

If you are unemployed or your employer does not offer health insurance, you may be able to continue health insurance for a limited time through your spouse's insurance plan under the federal COBRA (Consolidated Omnibus Budget Reconciliation Act of 1985) requirements or a state-mandated continuation program. You'll pay slightly higher premiums under COBRA, but the employer still administers the plan and the benefits do not change. COBRA is typically available for up to 18 months following a divorce, so it is not a permanent solution but can cover the period while you're waiting to get a job that includes insurance. Have your attorney confirm that COBRA coverage is available before final resolution of the case, and decide who will pay the premiums.

If you are not eligible for COBRA coverage, you can apply through the Texas health insurance risk pool. Check the requirements for this pool at www.txhealthpool.com.

Another option is to obtain coverage through an independent source. Depending on your financial situation, you can ask that your spouse pay the premiums for a specified period although, like alimony, this can be difficult to get a judge to order.

Many insurance companies do not cover pre-existing conditions. So if you have a major health concern and need to find new insurance, look into what expenses the new insurance will cover and examine this issue closely in relation to the division of your assets. Cancer and other major illnesses can play havoc with your financial situation. The costs associated with the illness and the limitations the illness can place on you may tax your ability to earn a living.

Heated disputes can surround serious health conditions. The husband of an ill wife may argue that she is not really sick but is making up the illness to get sympathy. To refute this claim, the wife's attorney may have a physician testify about her condition and its impact on her ability to work. Expert testimony is expensive, but if a large amount of money is at stake it might be a worthwhile investment. If you find yourself in this situation, you can reduce the cost by helping your attorney get copies of your medical records. Otherwise, your attorney may have to subpoena the records at considerable expense.

Life Insurance

If you or your spouse have an ongoing financial obligation after the divorce, such as child support or alimony, experts recommend that the one making the payments purchase a life insurance policy to cover the payments in the event of his or her death. "Having a life insurance policy in place gives a sense of confidence and security to both parties, and it leaves the person's estate in place to be distributed as planned," says financial planner Dave Patterson. "However, you don't need to establish a new policy. You can specify that some portion of an existing policy serves this purpose by changing the beneficiary information to designate that a certain percentage of the policy goes to the ex-spouse or the children."

Typically, the amount of the policy needed is determined by multiplying the dollar amount of the payments by the number of months the payments are expected to continue and adjusting that figure for inflation if necessary.

The settlement agreement needs to specify that the obligor spouse cannot modify the policy or diminish its value in any way, by loan, pledge, assignment or reduction. Often if children are involved, one spouse may require that the other establish a trust for the proceeds of the life insurance. Under such a trust, the obligor spouse specifies a trustee — normally the former spouse or a family member — who will use the life insurance proceeds for the benefit of each child. The trust usually states that the trustee will distribute any remaining proceeds to the children when they reach a specified age. Usually that age is 18, but it can be older.

17

What You Should Do With the House

DECIDING WHAT TO DO with your house may be the biggest decision you will face during your divorce. You have many options. We go into some detail on this subject, so carefully examine each option from a financial standpoint as well as from an emotional level. Remember that you're not just talking about a house; it's your home. You've shared good and bad moments there. You may have raised your children in it. If your gut reaction is to keep the house for your kids, you are like many people in your situation. But most divorced couples find it financially difficult to maintain a house if they struggled to afford it together.

Research your options and find out what you'll be able to afford on your own and decide what you really want. Realizing now that you do not want the house or cannot afford it is better than finding out after your divorce is final and you've made a difficult financial commitment.

These are your basic options:

- Sell the house
- Keep the house yourself
- Transfer the house to your spouse
- Stay in the house temporarily (you or your spouse)

How Important is the House?

Ask yourself if you want to stay in the house and why. In the end, the financial reality can overrule your emotions, but it's a good idea to decide if you even want to keep the house before you worry about whether you can afford it or not. You may feel the house contains memories you don't want to lose. After the divorce, constant reminders of the time spent with your ex in the house may prompt you to wish for a change of scenery. Sometimes a fresh start in a new place can help you move on. It's important to set yourself on a positive path, since what you're going through is difficult. Try not to saddle yourself with more emotional and financial baggage than you can handle.

You might worry that your kids need stability and removing them from their home would put an unnecessary strain on them, but kids are resilient. "It's more important to retain the child's relationships than it is to keep them in the same house," says Dr. Richard Warshak, a clinical psychologist and author of *Divorce Poison: Protecting the Parent-Child Bond from a Vindictive Ex.* "If the move allows the children to keep the same friends and school activities, that minimizes the negative impact."

You can also come to an agreement with your spouse that one of you stay in the house with the kids until you reach a good stopping point. People often want to wait until their kids graduate from high school.

"Looking for houses within the same school district is pretty easy these days," says real estate agent Saundra Stephens-Woodmansee. "Most agents can search the listings by school district and give you a list of the houses within the district that's in your price range."

Many school districts have more than one elementary, junior high and high school. So it's possible to find a house within the same district but outside your child's school zone. "When that happens, most cities allow your child to remain in the same school as long as the school isn't overcrowded and your child doesn't have attendance or discipline problems," says real estate agent Penny Bradshaw. "The fees for a transfer are minimal, often $25 to $50 per year. The only downside is that there may be no bus service, so you'll have to provide your own transportation."

Once you consider all the emotional reasons to keep or sell the house, it's time to think about the financial ones. If you and your spouse bought the biggest and best house you could afford, chances are you cannot handle it on your own and your spouse may not either. The mortgage, real estate taxes and homeowner's insurance are not the only things to consider in your calculations. The house will also need basic maintenance, lawn mowing and cleaning, not to mention emergency repairs such as heating or air conditioning. Granted, you'll have these expenses in any house, but a house is a bit like a car. The more expensive the car, the more expensive the upkeep and maintenance. A bigger house and yard requires more time and money than a smaller one.

Consider Your Housing Options

Gather as much information as you can about your options. It's better to have all the facts before you start making decisions. Don't assume anything. Some people put their homes on the market and then go house hunting, only to find that nothing in their price range is available where they want to live. This may not matter if you'll be living alone. But if you are trying to keep your children in the same school district, it can make a huge difference.

You'll probably have a change in lifestyle after your divorce, at least for the first couple of years. That may mean living in a smaller home or tightening your budget. Sometimes even though it's a stretch, it's better to keep the current home. If you've done the research, at least you will make an informed decision, which makes the burden easier to bear.

To find out what kind of house you could afford if you did move, sit down with a mortgage professional. Even if you don't know exactly how much income you'll have, a good mortgage loan officer can work with ballpark numbers and give you a general loan size, monthly payments and price range for house hunting. After you've figured out the numbers, it's time to sit down with a real estate agent, explain what you're looking for, drive through some neighborhoods and maybe even tour a few houses. "Many people only think about the amount of the new house payment when they're house hunting," says Stephens-Woodmansee. "They forget that they'll need to pay closing costs on both houses, the one they're selling and the one they're buying."

Try to formulate answers to the following questions:

Financial Questions
  • How much can you spend on housing each month? (rent, mortgage, insurance, taxes, condo or neighborhood association dues)
  • How much will you have for a down payment?
  • How large a loan amount do you qualify for?
  • What price range can you look in while house hunting?
  • How much money will you need for closing costs, moving and immediate improvements?

Real Estate Questions
  • What type of housing will fit your new lifestyle? (house, condo, apartment)
  • How much space do you need?

- Do you want to stay in your current school district?
- What areas would you like to live in?
- What is the price range of housing in those areas?

Selling the House

If you decide to sell the house, you do not need to hire a real estate appraiser. You can split the proceeds from the actual sale of the home, which can be higher or lower than the appraised value. If you and your ex cannot agree on a real estate agent, each of you should select an agent and have those two agents select a third agent to represent you. "Once you've found an agent, it often works best for that person to meet separately with each spouse," says Stephens-Woodmansee. "That way you're each getting the information directly, which prevents either of you from distorting the details of conversations to suit your own wishes."

After you've agreed on an agent to sell the house, have a title search done on your home. This search shows what liens exist against the property. Mortgages and home equity loans are liens you probably already know about. You're looking for the existence of any other liens, such as contractor or IRS liens. These will either be deducted from the proceeds of the sale of the home or need to be resolved prior to the sale if you decide to dispute them.

Your settlement agreement needs to address the following questions regarding the sale of your house:

- How will you divide the proceeds of the sale?
- How will you handle any tax consequences of the sale?
- Who will pay for the mortgage, taxes, insurance and utilities until the sale?
- Who will handle and pay for routine maintenance and upkeep until the sale?
- Who will handle and pay for any repairs and improvements to prepare for the sale (painting, roofing, etc.)?

- Will any of the above costs be reimbursed out of the proceeds of the sale (mortgage, maintenance, repairs, etc.)?

Your settlement agreement needs to specify that when you sell the house, you will deduct the following items from the gross sales price:

- The outstanding mortgage
- Any outstanding home equity loans
- Any other liens on the property
- Real estate agent's commission
- All closing costs including title policy
- Any legal fees related to the sale
- Cost of any repairs or improvements (depending on your agreement)
- Any other related terms of the settlement agreement, such as the payment of another debt

One of the biggest obstacles to selling a house can be one of the spouses. If one of you is not ready to let go of the house or truly doesn't want to sell, it's easy to throw up roadblocks to the sale. "Often one spouse or the other drags his or her feet when it comes to signing the paperwork and getting the house ready to show," says agent Penny Bradshaw. "We've even had cases where the judge had to issue a court order to one spouse to sell the home so we could get things moving."

Bradshaw says a few years ago she worked with a couple who wanted to see a house a divorcing couple was selling. "We scheduled an appointment to see the house, but when we arrived the woman said she hadn't gotten the message and wouldn't let us in. She said to schedule another appointment for the next day. As I was trying to retrieve the key from the lock box the next day, the wife came up the driveway screaming at me not to show the house. I was thoroughly confused since the woman had told me to reschedule.

She kept saying, 'You don't understand, this doesn't work for us.' Apparently, the husband was going bankrupt and the wife's name wasn't on the mortgage, so she was living there free, just waiting for him to go under, and wouldn't let anyone in to see the place."

Keeping the House Yourself

If you can afford it, you may be able to keep the house as part of the settlement agreement. To do this, you'll have to agree on a value that you can use in the division of your property. While you can determine a value on your own, you may get a more accurate number by enlisting the help of a real estate appraiser.

Sometimes couples cannot agree on the appraised value of their house, even after hiring a professional. You might worry that your spouse has influenced the appraiser to return a higher or lower value that benefits him or her in the division of your assets. Appraisers are licensed by the state and must follow certain guidelines when calculating the value of a house. Appraisals are not an exact science, though, so there is room for differing opinions. If you disagree with the value your spouse proposes, you can resolve the dispute by each selecting an appraiser, then having those two independent appraisers select a third appraiser who determines the value. You will probably have to pay a fee to each appraiser involved.

You may want to keep the house, but you should think carefully about whether this is truly the right decision. If you sell the house after the divorce and you haven't addressed the sale in the settlement agreement, you will have to pay all costs associated with the sale rather than splitting those expenses with your spouse. If you think only a few thousand dollars is at stake, think again. Most realtors charge 6% of the home's selling price. Added to closing costs, that eats up a large chunk of the proceeds you'll receive at the closing. However, those are not the only costs. Getting houses into selling shape sometimes requires maintenance and repairs that can cover anything from painting the walls to replacing the roof.

After you have agreed to keep the house, you'll want to get the mortgage into your name only. Most mortgage companies will not let you remove a name from the mortgage, so this can be a difficult task to accomplish. One way to achieve this is to refinance the mortgage in your name if you can qualify for the mortgage on your own. Keep in mind that a refinance is a new mortgage, so you'll have to pay current interest rates, closing costs and other fees.

If you keep the house and need to give your spouse his or her share of the equity because there are not enough assets to equalize the division of property, you can give your spouse a real estate lien note secured by a deed of trust with owelty lien. The terms of the payment should be addressed in the settlement agreement and the note.

Transferring the Residence From One Spouse to the Other

If one spouse is going to keep the home, the settlement agreement should specify that the other one must transfer all of his or her interest in the residence by signing a special warranty deed at the time the divorce decree is entered. The agreement should also specify who pays the mortgage and the real estate taxes. If you keep the house but your spouse agrees to pay the mortgage, the settlement agreement and divorce decree should characterize those mortgage payments as alimony enforceable by contempt or specify some other means of security in the event your spouse has a change of heart and stops making the payments.

Temporary Use by One Spouse

One of you can stay in the house for a specified period of time before selling it. This strategy is common among couples who have children in school and wish to plan the move around the school schedule. For example, if you have one child who is a junior in high school and another who will enter high school in two years, you might decide to stay in the home for those next two years. At this point, the older child will finish high school and you can move during the summer before the younger one switches to a new school.

If you choose this option, follow much of the advice listed for both keeping and selling the house. This is essentially a combination of the two. Your settlement agreement should contain all of the items listed above in "Selling the House," as well as how long you or your spouse will stay in the house and what events trigger the sale or what date the arrangement expires. "One strategy we've used in the past," says Stephens-Woodmansee, "is to specify in the settlement agreement that if we are offered at least X amount of dollars for the house, they'll take it. We always try to get more, but this establishes a base level for agreement so that one spouse can't continue to delay the sale indefinitely."

The main difference here concerns dividing the equity once you sell the house. If, for example, you live in the house for three more years and during that time you pay the mortgage and maintenance costs, you will probably want to keep the additional equity earned in the period after the divorce. You can deal with this by establishing a value at the time of the divorce, then subtracting that amount from the eventual sale price. Your settlement agreement should address what happens to any increase or decrease in value.

You'll also need to decide who holds the title and the mortgage during this time. If your spouse stays in the home, you may not want to transfer your interest because you'll lose leverage in forcing the sale and getting your share of the equity if your spouse later decides not to sell. However, if you prefer to have your spouse refinance the mortgage and want to transfer title to him or her, your attorney can prepare a note for your spouse to pay you a specified amount and a deed of trust with an owelty lien for your spouse to sign in return. This allows you to foreclose if your spouse does not pay you.

Deciding to sell the house later can create complications, but you can handle them smoothly if everything is specifically and accurately set forth in the agreement.

Impact of Keeping the Existing Mortgage

If the mortgage is in both names, you will both remain on the mortgage unless the one who keeps the house refinances it alone or the lender agrees to release one of the parties. Keeping the mortgage in both names is usually not a problem for the one who keeps the house but can cause two major problems for the one who does not. Having this obligation in your name can make it difficult to qualify for a new mortgage. And the spouse who stays in the home can ruin the other spouse's credit if he or she stops making the mortgage payments on time.

When you apply for a loan, such as a mortgage or a car loan, the creditor requests a copy of your credit report and counts each debt on it as a monthly payment. If your name remains on the old mortgage, you may only qualify for a new loan if the creditor thinks you can afford to make the old payment and the new payment along with any other debts listed on your report. Some creditors will ignore the old mortgage payment if you show them your divorce decree, but many will not.

Though the divorce decree is a legal document, it does not release you from making mortgage payments as long as your name remains on the mortgage. If your spouse stops making payments and you fail to make them yourself, your credit can be damaged. A missed mortgage payment has a much greater effect on your credit than a missed credit card payment. Missing even one or two mortgage payments will affect your ability to qualify for any new credit and may raise the rates financial institutions charge you for years to come.

If your spouse keeps the home and your name must remain on the mortgage, your attorney can prepare a deed of trust to secure assumption, which allows you to foreclose on your spouse if he or she stops paying the mortgage. If you do not have this deed of trust, you can go to court to try to force your spouse to pay the mortgage or sell the house, but your credit may already be ruined by the time you get the situation resolved.

Tax Consequences

There may or may not be tax consequences associated with the sale of your home depending on how much money you gained from the sale and the period of time you owned it and lived in it. At the present time, you can receive up to $250,000 ($500,000 as a married couple) from the sale of a home you lived in without having to pay taxes on it or include it as income on your tax return, as long as you meet the ownership and use tests. In addition, you must not have excluded a gain from the sale of another home within the past two years. The ownership and use tests require that you owned and lived in the home for at least two of the five years preceding the date of the sale.[15]

Since these rules can get complicated and tax laws change from time to time, talk to an accountant about any potential tax liabilities associated with selling your house before you put it on the market.

Q&A

Will my spouse get any part of my separate property?

"In a Texas divorce, the courts do not have the right to divide or award a spouse's separate property to the other spouse. However, the court may consider the size of a spouse's separate estate when dividing community property."

Kristy Piazza
Family Law Attorney

18

Dividing Assets

ASSETS WITHIN THE CONTEXT OF DIVORCE are anything of value that you own. That value can be of a financial nature or a personal one. A restored classic car has a clear financial value, but the value of a shell of a car waiting to be restored may not be so obvious. To the right person, though, this could be an essential part of a treasured hobby. It's all in how you look at it. The task ahead of you is to divide everything you own. Every item will end up with you or your spouse or will be sold with the money included in the division.

Begin by compiling a complete list of everything you own. Your attorney can provide you with an inventory form that will jog your memory on different types of assets. Don't omit items like frequent flyer miles and personal collections. Both can carry a larger value than you may realize. Larger assets may have debts against them, so you must also decide if you will sell the asset to pay off the debt. If the asset isn't sold, it is usually best to award it to the spouse whose name is on the debt, since late payments will affect that spouse's credit.

Your attorney can help you determine the value of your assets, but only you can determine which assets are worth pursuing. In an ideal situation, you and your spouse can agree on most, if not all, of the property division.

Here is a list of common assets that you may own in addition to your family home:

- Real estate, such as land or rental property
- Stocks and bonds
- Checking, savings and money market accounts
- Life insurance
- Retirement plans (IRAs, 401(k)s, pensions)
- Stock options, deferred income and bonuses
- Business interests
- Patents
- Frequent flyer miles
- Automobiles
- Boats and trailers
- Furniture and furnishings
- Jewelry
- Antiques
- Artwork
- China, silver and crystal
- Family heirlooms
- Sporting equipment
- Personal collections, such as coins, stamps or guns
- Business equipment
- Tools and yard equipment

Community Property

Because Texas is a community property state, you and your spouse own equally all the assets you acquired during your marriage unless they are proven to be separate property. This concept originates from Spanish civil law, which considered the family a community in itself and an asset of the larger community. The idea was that members of the family should share property generated by the family.

Determining whether an asset is community property or separate property is an essential prerequisite to asset division. The court can only divide community property. All property that you and your spouse possess at the time of the divorce is presumed to be community property unless proven otherwise. Separate property remains with the one who can prove ownership and consists of:

- Property owned before marriage
- Property acquired during the marriage by gift or inheritance
- Property that can be traced to a separate property asset
- Recovery for personal injuries sustained by one of you before or during your marriage, except for any recovery for a loss of earnings during the marriage

All income earned during marriage, whether from separate or community property, is considered community property unless you agreed otherwise in a premarital or postmarital agreement. For example, if you had $50,000 in a brokerage account when you got married, any interest or cash dividends earned from that money during the marriage is community property.

Since separate property can easily become entangled with community property during the course of a marriage, establishing proof that an asset is separate can be difficult. If necessary, your attorney can hire a forensic accountant to trace separate property.

"People don't seem to have an appreciation for the magnitude or implications of the community property presumption," says forensic accountant Doug Fejer. "They think if they have money before they are married, naturally they'll get credit for it when they divorce. Proving that funds should remain separate can be difficult."

How the Court Divides Property

If you cannot agree about who gets what, the court will divide the property for you. Even though you own community property equally, the law does not require the court to divide it equally but provides for a "just and right" division of property. The court can consider the following factors for both you and your spouse when dividing your assets:

- Education
- Earning power
- Business and employment opportunities
- Differences in your income and earning abilities
- Physical health
- Age
- Need for future support
- Custody of your children
- Relative sizes of your separate estates
- Relative financial conditions and obligations
- Length of your marriage
- Fault in the breakup of your marriage (see Ch. 11)
- Benefits that the spouse who's not at fault would have received if the marriage had continued
- Dissipation of the community estate, such as excessive gifts to others or waste of assets
- Nature of the property to be divided
- Tax consequences
- Attorney fees
- Fraud on the part of either spouse

The factors are not so clear-cut and predictable as you might think. In one case where the couple used the collaborative law approach, the man came into the sessions with a superior attitude borne out of his years of success in business, years when his wife spent most of her time with her doll collection. The man was disdainful of her hobby, so he gave her most of the community property because it was obvious she would have difficulty making a living for herself after the divorce.

But things didn't turn out the way he expected. Soon after the divorce, the woman began trading parts of her collection and stumbled into a goldmine. For the next few years, she made more money than her ex-husband, buying and selling Beanie Babies.

You Should Decide

People often feel cheated when they lose the power to make decisions concerning their property. For this reason, it is usually in your best interest to work out an amicable division of property with your spouse. You know what you want, and you will take more time than the judge to consider who gets what. The truth is that a judge doesn't really want to divide personal items, so when you leave it up to a judge, he or she will deal with the property division quickly, as part of the resolution of the entire case, and you may not like the outcome.

One case showed how two people can split their own property no matter what is at stake. The man was a serious gambler, and his game of choice was the stock market. The couple had been married almost three decades and had amassed a sizeable estate, which consisted of almost $20 million in cash, some real estate and options to purchase stock in a speculative venture that was close to the gambler's heart.

He wanted those options, and he instructed his attorney to give up everything to retain control of the options because he was convinced they would be worth $100 million in five years. The attorneys crafted a deal whereby the wife got more than half of the other assets and would get 10% of any appreciation in the value of the options.

Q&A

Can I get part of my spouse's retirement plan?

"You are probably entitled to a share of retirement benefits accumulated by your spouse during the marriage. However, while some accounts are fairly easy to divide and transfer, IRA's for example, others require a special court order approved by the retirement plan administrator. If the plan allows for early withdrawal (assuming you need the money and aren't retirement age), you will get hit with a 10% early withdrawal penalty plus the income taxes on the amount you withdraw. Suddenly, you've lost a big chunk of the value. So, if you need money right away, a retirement plan may not be your best bet."

Charles Hodges
Family Law Attorney

Since the couple reached an agreement, they each got what they wanted. A judge might have divided their estate very differently. Instead, the wife was protected with hard assets and the man got to ride those options wherever they would take him. They never did pay off, but to a gambler the thrill of such an asset lies in the endless possibilities and the assurance that he was able to play the game. The man would have been extremely disappointed if he'd had to walk away without control of them.

If you don't get something you dearly want, it may be gone forever if your spouse does not want to trade it for something else of value. Even if you have some issues that you need to go to trial over, it's best to work out the property division yourselves.

Household and Personal Items

Household and personal items include furniture and furnishings, artwork, appliances, clothing and jewelry. Often attorneys ask a divorcing couple to divide their household and personal items and then move them to separate locations so the settlement agreement can state that they each keep the items in their possession at the point of signing.

If you cannot divide and physically separate the items before you sign a settlement agreement, then the agreement needs to list each item and who should receive it. Be specific. If you will receive one-half of the pictures in your residence, specify exactly which pictures are yours or a method for taking turns choosing them. Keep in mind that if you argue over household or personal items, you may spend more in legal fees to get the items than you would spend to replace them.

You must assess whether the emotional and financial cost of pursuing certain property is worth it. Many people admit later that they argued out of ego and pride rather than logic, and that in the end they did not even want the asset they won due to the bad feelings now associated with it.

Retirement Accounts

Retirement benefits can be one of the largest marital assets. Some retirement plans are worth more than the equity in your home. If you acquired the benefits during your marriage, they are part of your community property and are subject to division. The best course of action is to obtain statements showing the current value of each of your retirement plans before beginning any negotiations regarding the property division.

"You can divide retirement accounts, but if it's possible we generally try to give different assets to the other spouse in order to keep the retirement account in one piece," says financial planner Dave Patterson. "For example, one spouse might get to keep the home and its equity, along with the balance of the couple's savings accounts, while the other spouse keeps his or her retirement account intact."

Some retirement accounts were initiated before a couple married, so some of the funds are separate property and the rest are community property. "As a general rule in cases like this," says Patterson, "we simply find out the value of the account at the time of the marriage and subtract it from the total value of the account. Only the money accumulated after the marriage is community property. However, depending on the type of assets or accounts in question, a more complicated analysis may be necessary."

Spend some time verifying the value of your retirement plans and evaluating their tax implications. If an account's value is not readily available, your attorney can usually obtain the information necessary to value it from the account manager.

In some cases, there just aren't enough other assets in the marriage to offset the value of the retirement account. Your attorney, or an expert hired by your attorney, should understand the laws governing retirement plans and how to use a Qualified Domestic Relations Order (QDRO) to divide a plan. With a QDRO, you can split a plan into two separate accounts without incurring the usual penalties for early withdrawal. Once divided, though, each account is still subject to the usual restrictions and tax liabilities imposed on the plan.

Closely Held Businesses

If you or your spouse owns a business or an interest in one, your settlement agreement needs to specify who receives the business and how it will be managed after the divorce. Usually, one of you will get total control over the business, but some divorcing couples remain partners and continue to run the business together. If one of you receives the business, your agreement needs to specify whether the other is obligated for any previous debts or taxes, or if he or she will receive any of the ongoing profits of the company. It also needs to specify who will pay any future debts and taxes associated with the business. If the company is successful, you may want an independent audit of the books and records and a business appraisal to determine its true value before finalizing the settlement.

Divorcing spouses can play more tricks with the valuation of a family business than almost any other asset of a marriage. It's common for a spouse who runs a company to downplay its value during a divorce. For example, a business owner might claim the last three years were the best years ever for the business and it is now likely to suffer a significant decrease in income just at the precise moment the divorce is granted. Or an owner might claim that the market is off and sales are suffering. Since you may have difficulty discovering the true value of a business, consult with your attorney and decide if you should hire a business valuation expert prior to negotiating a settlement.

One owner claimed his company earned him only $20,000 in the previous year. The man's wife knew the business earned him as much as $250,000 each year. Using the owner's low-ball annual profit figure and assuming that his particular type of company was worth five times its annual earnings, the wife's attorney offered to purchase the business from the man for $100,000. The attorney also guaranteed to send him a cashier's check for that amount within three hours. The husband declined the offer, saying that a lot of factors go into valuing a business and, while it was a loser at the moment, he felt it had potential.

After raising the bid several times until it was more than twice the original offer, the man still refused. It appeared he had been practicing some creative accounting, and his refusal confirmed what they suspected. At that point, the woman and her attorney stopped bidding for the business and began to concentrate on discovering its true value. The overall settlement she received was much better than she would have gotten had she accepted his initial figures.

Wills and Beneficiaries

In the turmoil of divorce, people forget to think about wills and estate planning. Normally you cannot make changes to beneficiaries of insurance policies during the divorce, but you can prepare these documents and have the changes ready to go once the divorce is final. You can also work with a financial planner and an estate planning attorney to prepare a new will that goes into effect before the divorce is final. If you don't update these documents at the time of your divorce, you may neglect them indefinitely. In the event of your death, those left behind will have a difficult time trying to sort it all out. If your will still says that your assets go to your ex, that's probably what will happen, even if you have been divorced for several years.

Do not assume you covered everything by changing your will. You must also change any accounts with beneficiaries, such as insurance policies, qualified retirements plans and annuities. "Simply stating in your will that you want all of your assets to go to your children or your new spouse won't work," says Patterson. "A will cannot override the titling issues in an estate, which are the accounts with specific beneficiaries."

Work with your attorney and a financial professional to make sure you handle all of your financial issues at the time of the divorce, not just the items you divide with your spouse.

19

Dividing Debts

WHEN SPLITTING UP THE THINGS YOU OWN, the last thing you want to think about is debt. But if you don't address your debts specifically and carefully in your settlement agreement, they could haunt you long after your divorce. The agreement needs to specify exactly which debts each of you is responsible to pay after the divorce. Generally, each of you should pay the debts in your own name and then you'll have to decide who will take over each of your jointly held debts if they cannot be paid immediately.

Whenever possible, it's best to pay off jointly held debts or in some way transfer the debt into one name, because if one of you stops paying, the other person's credit suffers even if you've already been divorced for several years. You can specify in the settlement agreement that the one responsible for each jointly held debt indemnifies the other from any expense resulting from nonpayment of the indebtedness. But this is difficult to enforce, since the person probably stopped paying the debt due to lack of funds. If you sue your ex over it, there may not be any money to win and your credit would already be affected. Creditor's rights to pursue collections against both of you cannot be limited by your settlement agreement.

Specifically Which Debts?

The settlement agreement must clearly identify each debt so that there is no question who is responsible for each account. One poorly worded agreement stated, "The parties have certain debts and the wife shall pay two of the debts and the husband shall pay two of the debts." The couple most likely knew which debts they were supposed to pay, but if one of them stopped and the other had to take the dispute to court, a judge would have no way to enforce the decree with a statement as vague as this.

The first place to start when compiling a list of your debts is to get a copy of each of your credit reports from all three credit bureaus. The reports should list all debts, except business debts, that you and your spouse hold with financial institutions. New accounts can take up to three months to appear on your credit report, and new charges often take a month to appear, so some recent activity may not be listed. Some creditors only report to one of the three credit bureaus, which is why it's important to get reports from all three. Depending on what type of report you request, you may see duplicate entries where the same account is listed more than once.

Debts not listed on your credit report could include loans or other debts incurred through a business, money borrowed from friends and family and debts to small businesses that do not report to the credit bureaus.

Typical debts include the following:

- Mortgages
- Home equity loans
- Home improvement loans
- Personal loans
- Auto loans

- Boat loans
- Credit cards
- Furniture store loans or cards
- Department store cards
- Student loans
- Business loans
- Collections and judgments
- Loans from friends and family

Who's Responsible?

A creditor may hold you liable if your spouse does not pay a debt held in both your names. The court has no authority to order a creditor or mortgage company to release you from liability, even if your divorce decree says you are no longer responsible for the debt. If your spouse does not make the payments as ordered, you can take him or her to court on an enforcement action. The creditor can still seek payment from you, but you might be able to secure a judgment against your spouse or gain some other relief from the court.

Pay off as many jointly held debts as possible and cancel the accounts, or convert them into the name of the spouse who will be paying the debts. You can also specify in the settlement agreement that certain debts must be refinanced within a certain time to remove your name from the obligations. The agreement should also provide that if the refinancing does not occur, certain assets will be sold to pay the debts.

Factors Considered in Apportioning Debt

The court considers several factors when deciding who will be responsible for each marital debt. Some of the factors include:

- Whose name the debt is in
- The purpose of the debt

- Who will retain any assets related to the debt
- Your financial resources
- Any agreement between you concerning the debt
- Overall apportionment of your property
- Length of your marriage
- Fault in the breakup of the marriage

Provide your attorney with a list of the marital debts, including a breakdown of who incurred each debt and whose name is on each account. Include a detailed list of any purchases relating to the debts and the status of those assets. For example, if you bought bedroom furniture and are still paying it off, let your attorney know who will keep the furniture. Include the name, address and account number for each creditor. You can find this information on your account statements.

The court does not look favorably on a spouse who makes a large number of charges on joint credit cards immediately before separation or the filing of a divorce. As a result, you'll need to substantiate any recent charges as being reasonable and necessary.

Strategies for Dealing with Debt

One of the things couples argue about most is money, so it's not surprising that divorce only makes financial problems worse, often to the point of affecting your credit. Unfortunately, the strain of paying for two households and attorney's fees is not the only reason for financial difficulties. Some people use monetary matters as a means to punish their spouse and exact revenge.

One woman moved out but agreed to split the mortgage payment with her husband until the house sold. He continued to live in the house and although he had the money, he refused to pay the utilities because his name was not on the accounts and he could punish his wife through nonpayment. She was forced to pay two sets of utilities—the ones at the old home and those at her new home—in order to protect her credit. Eventually, her realtor went to his lawyer and said that to show the home to prospective buyers, the utilities had to be on even if the wife stopped paying. This move resolved the problem, but only after months of frustration.

Whether your financial problems are caused by your situation or by each other, it may be more important now than ever before to protect your credit. Good credit makes a huge difference when applying for mortgages, auto loans and credit cards after the divorce. Your credit rating also affects the interest rates you pay as well as your ability to be approved for loans in the first place. Homeowner's insurance companies, auto insurance companies and even some employers check credit now. If your credit is poor, you'll pay higher rates and might not get the loan or the job because of it.

Most lenders want you to communicate with them if you find yourself struggling to pay your bills on time. Call each of your lenders and explain your situation. Ask them if there is anything they can do to help, such as lowering your interest rate or deferring a payment without setting late fees or reporting you to the credit bureaus. Sometimes you can renegotiate the terms of your loan or refinance it. Obtaining a home equity loan or refinancing your mortgage is one common way to pay off debt, but be aware that most lenders will not do this if your house is currently for sale or has recently been on the market.

Credit counseling can help, but choose the company carefully. Not all are as helpful as their advertising depicts them to be. One that is helpful is the non-profit company CCCS (Consumer Credit Counseling Service), which has offices throughout Texas. They sponsor a debt management program to repay debts by restructuring your budget and negotiating with your creditors.

If your only option is to pay some of your bills late, make your payments in order of importance to your credit rating. Paying your mortgage late will hurt your credit more than paying a credit card late. Formulas for calculating credit scores continue to evolve and change, but in general, each type of account is given different weight. You should always pay mortgages and home equity loans first before all other bills that appear on your credit report.

Here are some basic types of accounts listed in order of importance to your credit rating:

- Mortgage
- Home equity loan
- Auto loans and other installment loans with set payments
- Credit cards, cellphones, and other unsecured revolving debt
- Department-store cards and other retail store cards
- Utilities

Insurance does not appear on this list because insurance is not a loan or an account that accrues debt, so it does not appear on your credit report. However, you should continue to pay your insurance so that your coverage does not lapse and expose you to financial risk.

Q&A

If she gets the house (or another secured asset), can I get off the note?

"Assuming that the wife is awarded the marital residence or other secured asset and both parties' names appear on the mortgage, the wife would need to refinance the residence in her own name to remove her former husband from the mortgage. The husband typically signs a special warranty deed to convey his interest to the wife. The wife executes a deed of trust to secure assumption, which allows the husband to remedy any delinquencies if she fails to pay the debt.

Clint Brown
Family Law Attorney

Some Say This Lawyer's Good, Others Lucky

"As a young lawyer, I once took on a woman's contested divorce case on a Friday, and it was set for trial the following Monday. By an odd stroke of luck, the husband had a criminal trial set for the same day, and so the judge postponed the divorce trial for six weeks.

"It seems the man and his children were Christmas shopping when another driver cut them off on the expressway. The husband, a powerful guy at about 240 pounds, followed the other car into a shopping mall parking lot, pulled the teenage driver out of his car and screamed profanities at him. Then, in view of several holiday shoppers, he pressed a snub-nosed .357 revolver against the terrified teen's head and threatened to blow his brains out.

"Despite eyewitness reports and other evidence, the husband steadfastly claimed mistaken identity on the stand. He was shocked when the jury returned a guilty verdict after only 45 minutes. In the sentencing phase, the husband wept bitterly, admitting his crime and saying alcohol made him do it. When the husband finished his surprising statement, the judge excused the jury, had the husband arrested and charged with aggravated perjury and continued the trial.

"Even more amazing, the husband insisted on going through with the divorce trial. I subpoenaed the judge in the criminal trial and had him recite the husband's statements and the incredible result. My client won custody of her children, thanks to the lucky break provided by her husband."

Rick Robertson
Family Law Attorney

Part Four:
Going to Court

20

Our Court System

ONLY A SMALL PERCENTAGE of family law cases make their way into the courtroom here or in other states, but plenty of preparation takes place on the chance that a case won't settle. Because of this uncertainty, it pays to know about the court system.

In Texas, divorces are heard through our system of state district courts, which are presided over by elected judges. In large metropolitan areas, some district courts handle only domestic relations cases, including divorces and child custody matters. The judges of these courts are often board certified family law specialists and deal exclusively with family issues. Some people confuse family courts with juvenile courts, which deal mostly with matters relating to minors, often in the criminal arena.

Dallas County, for instance, has seven family district courts that handle divorce matters. Tarrant County (Fort Worth) also has seven such courts, while Harris County (Houston) has nine. In these counties, each family district court also has an associate judge assigned to handle temporary orders hearings and other matters. The counties of Bexar (San Antonio) and Travis (Austin) do not have family district courts, so divorce cases are heard by civil district courts that handle many kinds of civil cases. Galveston, Gregg, Midland and El Paso counties each have one court designated as a family district court. District judges in the remaining counties hear many different matters, from business lawsuits to criminal matters to divorce.

Because of the differences in the way cases are heard in various settings, court procedures in Marfa out in the Big Bend country of West Texas can be different from those in more metropolitan Dallas or Houston. It always helps to familiarize yourself with the judges and the workings of the court in the jurisdiction where your case will go to trial. If you live in a rural county and decide to import a family law specialist from a larger city to handle your divorce, it usually helps to employ local counsel who can advise you and your attorney on local customs and court procedures.

Temporary Hearings

Setting the ground rules for how you and your spouse handle things until your divorce is final is an important first step in the process. You must decide where the children will live, who will live in the house, how much child support or spousal support will be paid and to whom, who will pay the bills and who will have the use of certain assets. In most instances, you can settle these issues between yourselves with the assistance of your attorneys. A phone call or two should put the process in motion.

Only the most contested cases need to resort to a temporary hearing to resolve these matters. Temporary hearings usually are held within 14 days after the divorce is filed. They are expensive and time consuming but may be necessary if you simply cannot agree. In the Texas counties with specialty courts, associate judges appointed as magistrates to assist family court judges handle most divorce-related pretrial activities. In jurisdictions that don't employ associate judges, the judges themselves decide temporary issues.

Courtroom Cast of Characters

Here are the titles and functions of the people you may encounter at the courthouse:

Judge: In Texas, the judge in a family court or a civil district court is an elected official who runs the courtroom. Depending on what issues are not agreed upon by the spouses, he or she can be the sole decision maker or preside over a jury trial where he or she makes only some of the decisions.

Associate Judge: This person helps the judge by presiding over temporary hearings and taking the place of the judge on some matters. This is an appointed position rather than an elected one.

Bailiff: This is a uniformed officer of the court who keeps order and enforces the wishes of the judge or master. If the judge holds someone in contempt, the bailiff may take that person to jail. In jury trials, the bailiff acts as a liaison between the jury and other court personnel, including the judge.

Court Clerk: This person manages the court's files, including handling all of the paperwork necessary to a hearing or trial and other paperwork filed with the court.

Court Coordinator: This person posts the court's docket and handles the scheduling of hearings and trials.

Court Reporter: This job is changing with advances in technology. Traditionally, a court reporter takes down everything said in court and prepares transcripts for later hearings, trials and appeals. Some jurisdictions are now beginning to computerize this function.

Judge or Jury?

In many contested divorces, the big question is whether you want a judge or a jury to decide your fate. Texas has a long tradition of allowing people their day in court before a jury of their peers, and Texas is the only state that extends this right to child custody issues. "Often people try a case to a jury when they anticipate the need for an appeal," says Dallas family court Judge Marilea Lewis. "You're more likely to win an appeal on a jury trial, because there are more places to look for flaws."

Juries have historically been more important in deciding the outcome of child custody cases than property cases. Sometimes a case is not strong on the finer points of the law but has a powerful emotional context. When that happens, trying your case in front of a jury full of parents and grandparents can work in your favor. These everyday folks know a loving, caring relationship when they see one. Since they don't deal with the difficulties of legal disputes on a daily basis, they are more likely to take the emotions of a case into account when making their decisions. Child custody issues you can submit to a jury include:

- Sole custody or joint custody?
- If joint custody is awarded, which parent has the right to designate the primary residence of the child?
- Do you impose a geographic restriction on the child's primary residence and, if so, to what geographic area?

The judge cannot disregard the jury's verdict on any of these issues. However, a jury cannot determine child support, terms or conditions of possession or access or the rights and duties of the parents.

In cases concerning community property, the judge makes the ultimate division, but a jury can decide the value of an asset or decide whether something is community or separate property.

A jury trial can easily cost double what a bench trial costs because of the additional time involved. "It takes longer to make arguments to a jury," says Judge Lewis. "With a jury you have 12 people in a box. They cannot work straight through like a judge can, because they lose focus and need more breaks. If you're using experts, the judges in family court are already familiar with most of the experts in the area and their terminology. All of this has to be explained to a jury. In terms of time spent, a three-day bench trial is roughly equivalent to a six-day jury trial. If you're paying your attorney by the hour, that's double the amount of hours."

You do not need to choose between a judge and jury until a judge is assigned to your case. Your attorney should be familiar with the judge and can advise you whether he or she might be sympathetic to your case or if you'd have a better chance with a jury. It is a complicated decision and one you need to discuss carefully with your attorney.

21

Preparing for Trial

IN DIVORCE, AS WITH MOST THINGS IN LIFE, those who come prepared have the best chance of winning. This principle extends from the preparation of witnesses and your theory of the case to the way you look and act on that important day.

"I can't emphasize enough the need for preparation," says Judge Lewis. "The attorney is only as good as the information given by the client. Being prepared means that you have an understanding of the extent of your estate, you are familiar with your children's schedule and you know the ups and downs of your case. If you know all of this, you're more likely to get your side heard."

Your lawyer will have a specific plan for handling your case at trial and should go over it with you beforehand. Ask your attorney to walk you through every step of what will happen and explain the relevant issues he or she will address each day. Be open to his or her every suggestion. Your attorney may even request that you attend a trial similar to yours so that you can get an idea of the intensity of the proceedings and what to expect from the opposing counsel and the judge.

Preparing to Testify

"You have to learn how to be a good litigant," says Dr. Jan De-Lipsey, a psychologist who specializes in social sciences and litigation consulting. "There is a special world of communication inside the courtroom that does not translate to the outside world. For example, answering a question directly with merely a yes or no might be considered rude or abrupt in the outside world, but inside the courtroom it's considered responsive and economical. Judges want cases processed quickly, so you need to learn how to communicate effectively in this environment. You also need to communicate feelings, thoughts and actions and speak from the heart about things that matter the most."

You and your lawyer will want to review the questions you may be asked on the stand and how you will answer each one. You must always tell the truth, but there are many ways to answer the same question. Rely on the experience of your attorney to determine the best way to reply. Don't give the opposing party any leverage, no matter how much you want to tell the whole story. Once you establish a fact, move on.

One man with a family history of high blood pressure recently had his doctor prescribe medicine for him. Several people in his family have died of heart attacks, but he is a healthy man in his mid-30s. In spite of that, he knew his wife's attorney would attempt to portray him as an individual too sickly to be left alone with their young son.

When the opposing attorney asked if he took blood pressure medicine, the man simply said yes. The attorney then asked him if he had heart disease. His answer was a firm no. Since he did not elaborate, he did not give the attorney information to use against him. The attorney could poke and prod through the man's family history. But since the man looked perfectly healthy, these questions would seem a needless invasion of his privacy and a waste of time.

An effective family lawyer should know how much or how little information a judge or jury needs to make a decision. Many people feel the need to explain every thought and action in boring detail. A good lawyer is keenly aware that too many irrelevant and repetitive details can frustrate the judge or jury. If you or your lawyer waste too much time covering needless facts, the judge or jury may turn any animosity felt for your spouse into anger at you for wasting their time.

Get Friends and Family to Court

One of the most distasteful aspects of a divorce trial is the need to persuade friends and family members to testify on your behalf. You may be quite able to articulate how good a spouse and parent you've been, but judges and juries tend to put more weight on what others say about you. The theory is that you are probably a good person if your friends and family risk alienating your spouse to make a point in your favor. In addition, friends and family are often the only ones who can corroborate claims you make about your spouse, such as physical abuse or a gambling addiction.

You never know how someone will perform on the stand, but you can often get a general idea by having your attorney speak with each person beforehand. In one case, an attorney planned to use the husband's neighbor and landlord as a character witness in a child custody case. All he hoped to establish was that the man paid his rent on time (financially responsible) and often played in the front yard with his son (good dad). During the interview, the attorney noticed that the neighbor appeared distressed. When he asked what was wrong, the neighbor blurted out, "What if they find out about my kids?" He explained that decades ago he had abandoned his own family and hadn't seen his children since. The attorney knew the opposing side probably wouldn't use precious resources to investigate such an unimportant witness, so the only way they would find out was if the neighbor told the story himself on the stand. Since the attorney didn't want to take that chance and already had plenty of character witnesses, he thanked the neighbor for his time and struck him from the witness list.

Work with your attorney to decide who will testify for you and what questions to ask. Rely on the expertise of your attorney to figure out who will help you, who might hurt you and who is extraneous to your case. You may not want to ask someone to come to court for you, especially when he or she knows your spouse and by testifying would risk losing a friendship. However, if your attorney thinks that person is essential to your case, it's your job to help get that person to court.

Get Plenty of Rest

Nothing causes sleepless nights like a contested divorce, especially when child custody is at issue. It is important, though, that you come to court fully prepared, which includes being rested and ready for the day ahead. Do what you can to take your mind off the proceedings the night before, like going to a movie or taking in a sporting event. Do not take a sleeping pill or drink alcohol to help you sleep better, as these things will leave you feeling groggy the next day. The proceedings are more likely to turn out in your favor if you walk into court feeling rested and in control.

22

Your Day in Court

FROM THE MOMENT YOU LEAVE YOUR HOME on the day of a court appearance, you are part of the court system and should be careful how you act. You never know who you'll run into and how your actions will affect the outcome of your trial.

One young wife and mother arrived late for a court date. She circled the courthouse, searching for a parking space and glancing nervously at her watch. A large sedan emerged from a side street and slowly pulled out ahead of her. She noticed that the driver, a short bald man, could barely see over the steering wheel. He was obviously in no hurry, as he too searched for a place to park, with the young woman stuck behind him.

Just then, she saw a car pulling out of a space on the street ahead. Her divorce trial was starting in five minutes. All she could think of was that a large estate and custody of her children were at stake. With no time to lose and her frustration level peaked, she pulled out and sped around the big sedan and into the parking space. The man had to brake quickly to avoid hitting her and drove by obviously perturbed.

Once inside the courthouse, she found the ladies' room where she checked her hair, straightened her suit and took a few moments to compose herself. Today was jury selection, and she wanted to look her best. She entered the courtroom quietly and sat down next to her attorney. When she looked up at the row of prospective jurors, her heart skipped a beat as she recognized the juror on the far left. It was the man she outraced to a parking space.

The Shifting Court Calendar

A case may be reset several times before it actually reaches trial, if it ever does. Continuances occur for a variety of reasons including each side's readiness to try the case, conflicts with the schedules of either party or their attorneys and conflicts with the court's docket. If you cannot settle your case, eventually it will be set for trial on the court's calendar. Nearly half of all cases filed in the courts of Texas involve some facet of family law, which means the court has many cases competing for its time.

When you arrive in court, it will probably be crowded with the people involved in a number of cases that may be set on the judge's docket for the same day. The hallways outside the courtroom are often lined with hard wooden benches filled to capacity with litigants, their witnesses and lawyers. Many family law cases are resolved right here at the last possible moment.

Usually the judge calls the docket first and checks the status of each case with the attorneys representing the parties. The attorneys may request a continuance, an opportunity to talk settlement or a moment to speak with the judge about a particular issue that needs clarification before the case can proceed. The judge will determine, based on the cases set that day, which ones will be heard.

The judge's determination of which cases to hear is based on a variety of factors. In courts that handle criminal cases, those usually come first if there are any on the docket. After that, or in courts that handle only family law cases, the case with the oldest filing date often takes priority. Sometimes the judge weighs the seriousness of the issues at hand. If there is an emergency issue on the docket — such as an immediate threat of family violence — the court usually attempts to resolve this issue, even if it is only a short-term fix. If the judge is already in a jury trial on a case from the previous day, it is normal to proceed with that case and reschedule the rest. This is how the judicial system works, and your lawyer cannot do much about it.

If witnesses must come from far away or other hardships make it difficult for someone to come to court, your lawyer can attempt to call the courthouse on the day before your trial to determine where you are on the docket and what kind of cases are set before yours. This tells you to some degree whether your case may go to trial. Court personnel vary according to the amount of information they will give, and some require that you show up at the courthouse every time your case is set regardless of what else appears on their docket. If your lawyer is an expert in this area, he or she should be able to tell you whether the judge and his office will help coordinate the scheduling of your trial.

How to Present Yourself

First impressions are important in all aspects of life, but they are especially important in custody or marital disputes where a judge or jury must evaluate your credibility. Your personal appearance and manner can have a huge impact, so it is worthwhile to spend some time on your appearance before going to court.

In the past, men and women were encouraged to wear suits. Today, in our more relaxed environment, casual business attire is generally appropriate. You should look more like a mom or dad, and less like one of the lawyers, unless you normally wear a suit every day for your profession. Stay away from jeans or flashy attire, and wear a conservative amount of jewelry. If you have any questions about your wardrobe choices, ask your lawyer.

Always act in a mature and professional manner in court. In past years, court personnel have witnessed numerous threats or actual harm in the courtroom. Judges are sensitive to any hint of violence and will not hesitate to remove the potential offender.

Always remain calm and cool, even if deep down you feel quite the opposite. Many cases have been settled because one spouse came to a hearing or trial with a poker face, which convinced the other side that he or she was not overly concerned about the outcome. If your spouse has been the dominant one in your marriage, following through with the drama of a trial can demonstrate that you are serious and will not settle for less than what is fair.

Keep Your Cool on the Stand

During any appearance before a judge or master, remain focused on the issues at hand. Sit up straight in your chair, speak clearly and be polite at all times. Remember that the judge (or the jury, if one is present) is evaluating your responses and your overall behavior to determine what kind of person you are. Do not be argumentative or hostile when the opposing attorney asks questions you don't like, and never answer in a haughty or sarcastic manner. Your attorney will object to inappropriate questions and make arguments when needed.

The time you spend answering questions from your attorney is when you establish your side of the case. The time spent under cross-examination is when most people show their temperament. Your spouse's attorney will ask you plenty of yes-or-no questions. In many instances, you'll want to elaborate, but yes or no may be all you are allowed to say because the opposing attorney will cut you off. For example, the lawyer might ask, "Have you ever yelled at your children?" Few people can answer no to this question, but when you answer yes, you'll probably have an uncontrollable urge to explain yourself. At this point, the attorney usually steps in and says, "Please just answer the question with a yes or no."

Lawyers use this strategy to frustrate people in an attempt to get them to lose their tempers and show the judge or jury a difficult person under the facade. This tactic can work on even the most calm and collected people, so prepare for it. A good family law specialist will practice with you beforehand, asking all the anticipated questions in the safety and comfort of the law office, until you respond as you should. Remember, what you say is important, but how you say it can mean even more.

Answer Truthfully and Concisely

When your spouse's attorney questions you, give truthful and accurate answers. Lying under oath is not only illegal but can ruin your credibility with the judge or jury. "Jurors will forgive a lot of things," says psychologist Dr. Jan DeLipsey. "But they do not like being tricked by attorneys or lied to by people on the stand. Jurors know that just because you had an affair doesn't mean you're a bad parent, but if they catch you lying about it, that will go against you more than knowing the truth." Work with your attorney in advance on the best way to answer questions designed to make you look like a bad parent or spouse.

Do not give more information than the other side requests. If the opposing side does not ask the appropriate questions, do not help them win their case by providing the information anyway. Apply this principle to every question. Once you answer the question as briefly as possible, be quiet and listen carefully to the next question. If you are unsure how to answer certain questions, discuss your concerns with your lawyer before court.

The truth can help or hurt you in ways you may not expect. One woman had an affair with a neighbor. Her husband suspected the affair but did not know who the other man was until the woman admitted it on the witness stand. Feeling it could only help his side if the neighbor's wife knew, the husband went to her and told her all about it. The two of them ended up in bed together.

The husband, thinking nothing of his own indiscretion since it happened after the fact, felt the need to publicly punish his wife as much as possible. So he arranged for his children, some relatives and several members of their church to be present in the court-room for the sole purpose of embarrassing her. In the meantime, the neighbor's wife confessed to her husband that she'd had sex to get even with him. When it all came out in the end, the woman's attorney had one major point in her favor. While both of them were guilty of sexual indiscretions, the woman admitted her faults on the stand, but her husband had not and was guilty of hypocrisy.

Basic Rules for Giving Testimony

Keep the following rules in mind when you are on the witness stand:

- **Always tell the truth.**
- **Listen to the whole question.**
- **Do not respond to the question until the attorney completes it and your attorney has had a chance to object if necessary.**
- **Take your time.**
- **If you forget the question, ask the attorney to repeat it.**
- **Answer only the question asked.**
- **If it is a yes or no question, limit your answer to yes or no and don't add anything to it.**
- **Answer verbally, distinctly and briefly.**
- **Do not try to outguess or outmaneuver the opposing attorney.**
- **Do not argue with the opposing attorney.**

Our Marriage, Just As I Pictured It

"A few years ago I had a client who was awarded several pieces of furniture from the marital residence in the final decree of divorce. The case had been particularly bitter and my client's wife had accused him of a number of things, including that he was obsessive and picky about everything.

"When he went to retrieve the furniture, which included many valuable antiques, he brought along an off-duty policeman. He also brought a camera and took a photo of each piece. To the casual observer, it was yet another example of his annoyingly detailed behavior, but the man figured that his wife would substitute cheap imitations for some of their valuable antiques, and he was right.

"He had, of course, taken photos of the real antiques at an earlier time. With the policeman as our witness, we succeeded in a contempt action against the wife. Ironically, the very behavior that she complained about got the best of her in the end."

Ike Vanden Eykel

Part Five: Once Your Divorce Becomes Final

23

After Your Case is Tried (or Settled)

AT SOME POINT IN THE PROCESS, your case will come to an end. If it ends with a jury returning a verdict and the judge announcing his or her rulings in the case, the attorneys then prepare a document called a final decree of divorce. This document spells out all of the terms and conditions of child-related matters and the division of property and debts in accordance with the court's decisions.

If you are among the vast majority of litigants who settle their cases by mutual agreement instead of by trial, the final decree of divorce usually includes language that makes your agreement binding on both of you to the extent permitted by law. Once the judge signs the decree, your agreement becomes a court order and is enforceable the same as if the court made the decisions.

No matter how your case ends, you should read and understand all the terms and conditions of the decree and any settlement agreements before you sign them. You will have to live by these documents in the future and can be held in contempt for not abiding by their terms. If you have questions or concerns, ask your lawyer to explain your rights and responsibilities. Emotions can run high during a divorce, so it is normal to forget some details.

After the judge signs your decree, you should write any deadlines on your calendar and put the decree in a safe, convenient place so you can refer back to it whenever necessary.

What's Next?

There are tasks to complete within the first few weeks after your divorce becomes final that will bring your legal and financial paperwork up to date and reflect the changes outlined in your divorce documents. See Appendix D, the Post-Divorce Checklist, on page 276. It includes the following:

- If you plan to appeal, there are strict time limits, so discuss the situation with your attorney immediately.
- Change your will, general power of attorney, medical power of attorney and medical directive.
- Prepare and file real estate deeds transferring property interests in accordance with your decree.
- Transfer titles or bills of sale to automobiles, boats or other property.
- If you use a Qualified Domestic Relations Order (QDRO) to divide any retirement accounts, forward it to the plan administrator.
- Prepare and file insurance forms to change beneficiaries for insurance policies.
- Make sure you have health insurance in force and provide any required COBRA notices to your employer.
- For women changing back to your maiden name, request a name change for your driver's license, social security card and passport.

- Inform creditors and others of address and name changes on accounts.
- Change your name and address on bank accounts.
- Request delivery of income withholding orders for child support collection.

If You Want to Appeal

Overturning trial court decisions in a divorce case is difficult and rare. That's why it is so important to prepare your case well and get what you need either through settlement or trial the first time around. Still, you have two main avenues available for post-judgment review and relief — a motion filed with the trial court and an appeal to a higher court.

You have the right to file a motion to modify, correct or reform the trial court's judgment or request a new trial if you are not satisfied with the court's decisions. Under Texas law, you have 30 days from the date of the court order to file this type of motion. In reality, these motions rarely succeed unless the court failed to consider a material fact in evidence or the court made a clear and distinct error in its ruling. With a motion to modify, correct or reform a judgment or for a new trial, you are asking the trial judge to admit that he or she made a mistake that needs to be corrected.

You also have the right to appeal the final judgment. An appeal is submitted first to the Texas Court of Appeals. There are 14 such courts located in various cities around the state, and the number of judges in each court ranges from three to 13. A three-judge panel from one of these courts hears your appeal. If you are not satisfied with the action of the appellate court, you can apply to the Texas Supreme Court to review your case. Unlike an appeal to the Court of Appeals, the Texas Supreme Court decides which cases it will hear. Appealing a divorce case all the way to the Texas Supreme Court is rare and expensive and can be very complicated. Such an appeal is a last-ditch effort to change the trial court's judgment. The majority of appeals fail because the requirements are very strict. Successful appeals usually deal with specific issues, such as the trial judge not allowing the testimony of an important witness. Relying on the appeal process to remedy an injustice that occurred at trial is possible, but it's a long shot.

Uncovering Deception

Occasionally, one spouse hides an asset to keep it from becoming part of the property division in the divorce. If the other spouse finds the hidden asset after finalizing the divorce, he or she can petition the court to reopen the case and reconsider the overall settlement in light of the new information.

If certain kinds of fraud take place during the divorce proceedings that are not discovered until after the divorce is final, the trial court judge can set aside the division of property. The length of time you have to bring such a cause of action varies depending on the facts of the case. Your attorney can explain these complicated procedures to you if you believe your spouse has committed this type of deception.

24

Enforcing Your Decree

EVEN THOUGH YOUR DIVORCE DECREE should outline exactly how to handle things, you still have to figure out how to live with it. Sometimes as our roles and relationships change, past agreements or rulings no longer fit our situations.

This was true for the Maisal family. Melvin Maisal was the provider and he called most of the shots. His wife, Karen, stayed at home, took care of the children and assisted in his climb up the corporate ladder. At least that's how things worked until Melvin decided he wanted a divorce.

Karen felt confused and doubtful about this decision, but she made her way through to a settlement that everyone considered generous. She would not need to work unless she wanted to, and the lives of her children would continue as close to normal as possible.

Since the divorce was Melvin's idea, he felt obligated to give her the house and plenty of money. He also gave her complete authority over the children, although he assumed he would steer her in all the important decisions, because that is what he had always done.

At first, Karen went along with whatever Melvin suggested just as she had during the marriage. As their marriage receded from memory, though, she expressed her independence by making big decisions on her own. Soon she wanted to move to another part of the city, which meant the children would switch schools. Melvin objected to the move and was perplexed and incensed that she would question his authority. That began a pattern of bullying by Melvin and resistance by Karen that lasted for years.

Flexible or By the Book

Only you and your former spouse can determine whether you consider your decree set in stone or simply a guideline for your future. As your children grow and change, you'll need to decide how stringently to adhere to your decree. If your ex continually suggests changes to the daily routine, ask yourself the following questions:

- Is this change better for the children?
- Can it bother me or hurt me? Is it a short-term benefit but a long-term problem?
- If I agree to this change, will it become the foundation for something else that I do not want?
- Can I trust my ex to make this change unofficially, or do we need to go through legal channels?

There are no hard and fast rules to determine how much to stray from the plan laid out in your divorce decree. After several years, many divorced couples' lives bear little resemblance to what they imagined life would be like when their children were small. A follow-up story in *D Magazine* on a child custody case our firm handled summed it up best:

"In our case, a cute little white-haired preschooler would grow into a 6-foot-tall, 210-pound mountain of hormones, complete with car keys, girlfriends and responsibilities. And parents who divorced

each other long ago would find that, like it or not, they still had a relationship. Only in a few very extreme cases does the 'losing' parent
just go away and leave the children's welfare to the former partner.
The vast majority of cases, however bitterly contested, involve two
dedicated parents who settle into an awkward détente — not really
together, not really apart."[16]

Divorced parents who successfully raise their kids as they grow
and mature make many changes. They always try to act in the best
interests of their children and truly want the best situation for everyone involved. It takes time for the healing to begin so that you
and your ex can learn to work together as parents again. You can let
your anger rule your life, always checking your watch when your ex
is due to arrive with the kids, or you can use compassion and common sense to find your way.

Take Stock of Your Situation Each Year

It's worthwhile at least in the first several years after your divorce to set aside a specific time each year to consider how your
divorce decree is working and whether it is helping you manage the
daily lives of your children and yourself. In some cases, it may be
appropriate to see your attorney for an annual checkup. Let your
attorney know how things are going, if the visitation schedule is
working, how your children are doing, if child support is being paid
on time and the status of any other arrangements that stem from
the divorce. This is also a good time to ask questions that have aris-
en since your last conversation.

Here are some questions that might arise as your life goes on:

- My ex just got a better job. Can we get more child support?
- My ex wanted nothing to do with the children after the divorce. Now he wants visitation. What should I do?
- My ex's parents want to visit the kids, but I don't want them
  in my house. Any suggestions?

- I have a chance to help my career by moving to Los Angeles, away from my kids. How can I maintain contact?
- I am thinking about remarrying. What are the ramifications?
- I believe my ex hid some assets at the time of the divorce. Can we go back to court to recover them?

Just because your divorce is over doesn't mean you no longer need legal advice, which could help you get increased child support payments, receive a recommendation to a mental health professional for a troubled child or a referral to an attorney in another field to handle an unrelated legal matter.

Give and You Shall Receive

A little generosity can go a long way in a divorce. Nothing requires you to give more than you expect to receive. Yet on the whole, people who act in a reasonable manner reach settlement more readily and get special consideration in family court. This attitude extends beyond money to your time with your children as well.

One man, a father of two, agreed to pay $1,200 a month in child support, which was slightly more than the required amount. As time went on, he also picked up the cost of music lessons and tuition to a music camp for his kids, along with other miscellaneous costs he was not obligated to pay. When the man asked to extend his regular weekend visitation to allow the children to sleep over on Sunday night, his ex-wife refused.

Under the law, child support itself is not tied to visitation. But in court, the man's generosity emerged as a central theme. Besides consistently providing more money, he had willingly agreed to let the ex-wife use his lake house for her family reunion. He also stood by her when she had a surgical procedure and needed extra help with the kids. Over the ex-wife's objections, the court granted the man his extra night of visitation.

This story just goes to show that in dealing with the family courts, reason and generosity usually trump blind inflexibility and give you an extra card to play when necessary. It will make your children respect you more and may even make the relationship with your ex better over the long haul.

Contempt Actions

Generosity can't smooth over every problem. Sometimes your spouse simply won't comply with the divorce decree. When this happens you may need to file a contempt action to force compliance. Contempt can be used to enforce child custody and visitation orders, the payment of child support, certain types of financial and property matters and attorney's fees in some instances.

The standard for contempt is fairly simple. One spouse must willfully refuse to comply with a specific order of the court that is central to the obligation in question. For example, if your ex fails to pay child support even though he or she earns enough money to pay it, your spouse can be held in contempt of court. Likewise, you or your spouse can be held in contempt for failing to comply with a visitation schedule.

If the spouse paying child support loses a job and has no other means of paying the support, resolution of this issue would depend on the circumstances surrounding the failure to comply with the decree and the person's ability to explain the job loss.

Filing a contempt action asks the court to put your ex in jail or impose a fine for his or her failure to comply with the decree. Sometimes this drastic action is necessary to show that what the judge ordered wasn't merely a suggestion, and that you will not tolerate actions to the contrary. Jail time is a serious matter, though. Before you request it, ask yourself if you really want your children's other parent put in jail. Sometimes it is the only way to get what you need, but you should weigh the seriousness of your ex's contempt against the reality of jail time.

When a person is placed in jail, he or she gets released by serving the time or purging the contempt action, such as by paying the child support owed. The judge may issue an order of commitment to send someone to jail and then suspend the commitment as long as the person does certain things, such as make timely payments toward child support or return the children on time at the end of visits. Then, if the person does not comply with the terms for suspending the commitment, the court revokes the suspension and orders the person to serve jail time.

You can often predict problems with compliance early in the case. Spouses will sometimes make threats to withhold child support or keep the children for more than the specified visitation period. Take these threats seriously, but don't overreact. Wait until it actually happens. Always keep detailed records of support payments paid or received, plus violations of the visitation schedule, so that if a contempt action is brought, you'll have proof to back it up.

Only you can decide when being flexible and generous is worthwhile and when you need to stand up for yourself and the needs of your children. With an ex who doesn't take his or her responsibilities seriously, you must establish that you will not tolerate missed child support payments or allow the ex to return or pick up the children late.

Give your ex adequate time to comply before filing a contempt action, but don't wait too long. Many people wait until their ex owes them tens of thousands of dollars or a visitation problem has festered into a real fight before filing an action. Keep in mind that even if a contempt action for missed child support payments succeeds, you're unlikely to get a lump sum of money and may have to accept installment payments until your ex catches up.

25

Changes Regarding Children

THE MOST COMMON MODIFICATIONS to a divorce decree involve child custody, child support, visitation and relocation. Modifications can be expensive and disrupt lives, and you cannot request a modification simply because you did not like the outcome of the divorce. The requirement for almost any modification is that a "material and substantial change of circumstances" has taken place since the last court order concerning the aspect to be modified. This means that a basic change has occurred in the lives of the parents or the children, which justifies a modification of the terms of the divorce. Modifications are most difficult to obtain within the first year after the order you are seeking to modify.

Think long and hard about returning to the court system for a modification. Consult with your attorney to determine if it's necessary to make the changes legally or if you can accomplish what you want in another way. You must also determine if the positive effects of the modification will offset the negative effect of going back to court.

Change of Custody

Although joint custody is the preferred parenting arrangement in most Texas courts, it does not necessarily mean equal parenting and conflicts commonly will arise. Sometimes the conflicts become so severe that one parent seeks to modify the terms of a joint custody arrangement. A change of primary custody is the most drastic and difficult form of modification to a divorce decree. The parent asking for this modification must show a material and substantial change of circumstances and that the modification would be in the best interest of the child.

Do not request a custody modification simply because of a conflict with your ex. For example, if your ex has begun a new relationship or remarried, this alone does not justify a modification. A real reason must exist that warrants the change. If the parent who has the child during the week cannot get the child to school on time, it may make sense to determine if the other parent is better suited to perform that function. If the custodial parent develops a drug or alcohol problem or fails to get medical care for the child, that might necessitate an alteration in custody.

Sometimes one parent does not feel ready to assume the role of primary custodian at the time of the divorce or doesn't think the court would rule in his or her favor. In these instances, one parent may ask for joint custody and then wait to see how the other parent handles the new arrangement. Patience is essential in these matters. If sole custody is your ultimate goal, you may need to wait a year or two after the divorce to see how everyone settles into their new roles.

The judge or jury wants to know what is in the best interest of the children when determining whether to change the children's primary custodian or modify other terms of the custody order. Under Texas law, the economic resources of the parents cannot be the only consideration. Therefore, if your financial situation suddenly improves, that alone is not a reason for a change in custody. Under state law, living in a million-dollar mansion doesn't benefit a child more than living in a mobile home. Improved finances may justify an increase in child support rather than a change in custody.

To determine the children's best interests, the court looks at a number of factors, including:

- The overall performance of the children in the home of the primary custodian, including attendance and grades in school and general health
- What the children want (the importance of this depends on age and maturity level)
- Activities and friends of the children
- Stability of each parent and their home lives
- Abilities of the parents to provide time and other resources for the children
- Parents' work and travel schedules

Custody cases usually begin with an evaluation by a social worker affiliated with the courts or by an independent psychologist. Most urban counties have at least one court-affiliated counselor who studies the families and their households and reports their findings to the court. Most modifications are scheduled for mediation, and a great number are settled out of court. Changes of custody are difficult, though, and many people find they cannot change the conditions in which their children live.

Sometimes the way you approach the original proceeding affects the outcome of the modification action. For example, it is surprising how many parents agree to give an abusive parent joint custody or substantial visitation rights. Later on, it can be difficult to convince a judge to limit the other parent's access when you've known all along that abuse occurred.

Evidence presented in support of your request to modify custody must concern matters that occurred after the last order of the court regarding custody in your case. The trial judge often will not allow you to dredge up complaints you did not bring forward before the prior order was signed. Only in narrow circumstances, such as when showing a continuing course of conduct, are you allowed to present prior evidence.

Before you decide to try for a modification, think about the following questions and discuss them with your attorney:

- How will this action affect my child?
- How will it affect me and other family members?
- Can I count on friends and family members to help me with this, including testifying in court if necessary?
- Am I prepared to invest the time and money to accomplish this?
- Can I afford it?
- What is the best outcome I can reasonably expect and what's the downside of taking action?
- What will happen if I don't pursue this action?

Joint custody and the mediation process are responsible for reducing the number of full-blown custody trials, but trials still take place when an irreconcilable issue is confronted or when one parent tries to play hardball with the system. Custody trials are expensive and can divide families and friends, but winning a modification of child custody can be the most rewarding of all parental actions if your child's quality of life is at stake.

Child Support Modifications

A financial windfall received by either parent after the divorce should benefit the children just as it would if the family was intact. Both parents have a duty to support their children as best they can, so increases in the paying parent's income can justify a modification in child support payments. Conversely, if the paying parent loses a job or experiences a significant decrease in income, the amount of child support may be reduced. Periodic changes in the child support guidelines may also be a reason for modifications.

If a parent pays for expenses and activities over and above the mandated child support obligation, you may not want to risk having those extra payments discontinued by fighting for a slight increase in mandated payments. Any divorce attorney can calculate the projected amount of the new child support payments if you know the gross monthly income of the paying parent and the cost of health insurance premiums for the children.

Sometimes parents take defensive actions when called on to pay more child support. For example, the noncustodial parent may seek primary custody in response to the filing of a modification action for more child support. The court may realize that this is an effort to avoid paying higher child support, but the action can still create considerable problems and expense for the custodial parent who seeks the added support.

Additionally, if your conduct since the divorce can be called into question, you may not want to ask for a modification. For example, living with a new romantic partner may not seem like a big deal, but it may cloud the issue of child support and lead to a counter-petition by your ex for custody of the children. Every action in family court has an equal and opposite reaction. Modifications give rise to many reactions that you might not anticipate.

Modifying Visitation

The preference in the courts and in society is for good parents to have as much access to their children as possible. After the heat of divorce has cooled, many parents manage children's schedules between themselves. Informal modifications are common, but they aren't enforceable by law. Most parents find that as their children get older, a little flexibility is required. This kind of cooperation is recommended as long as you feel comfortable with the changes.

Quite often, the changes involve granting a noncustodial parent more time with the children. A teenage child may want to take a long trip or spend an entire summer with the other parent because they share a mutual interest. Some changes are simply refinements to the visitation schedule. For instance, instead of returning the children on Sunday night, the noncustodial parent may keep the children through Monday morning and drop them off at school. Consider each request carefully, keeping in mind the needs of the child, the ability of the other parent to accept this responsibility and how the changes may affect your future rights.

Sometimes changes in visitation are necessary because one parent has an adverse affect on the children. "If your children seem to be harmed by spending time with your ex and they're not getting better, that can be an indication that you need to get the legal system involved again," says clinical psychologist and author Dr. Richard Warshak. "You may need help if your ex frequently tries to intervene during your time with them, for example, constantly planning activities that conflict with your visitation schedule or repeatedly calling the children when they are with you." These are often indications that your ex is intentionally trying to disrupt the lives of you and your children, and you may have to request a modification to the visitation schedule to stop the behavior.

Social workers in family court services often recommend visitation changes after they interview the parents and other necessary family members. Modifications to schedules, like other modifications, are expensive to achieve if you go to court to achieve them. You will likely spend at least several thousand dollars to get one additional evening of visitation or deny your ex that amount of time with your children. Remember, your children invariably get older and circumstances change. If you and your ex can remain flexible and reasonable about your schedule, you will avoid a lot of heartache and expense down the road.

Relocation

A parent with sole or primary custody wanting to move with a minor child to another city or state is often one of the most contentious types of modifications. Attorneys, psychologists and social scientists have varying opinions when it comes to this issue in terms of what is in the best interest of the child and whether a person's right to move should be restricted by the courts.

Due to the increased mobility of our society, many states, including Texas, are struggling with this issue, especially since the shift toward granting joint custody has led to an increase in residence restrictions imposed in the decree of divorce. A primary custodial parent who is restricted to living in a particular area so that the child can maintain relationships with both parents must return to court if he or she wants to move beyond the area. At present, the law requires that each situation be reviewed on a case-by-case basis but the parent who requests the move must provide a compelling reason for doing so.

Consider all the factors when deciding to relocate. If the distance is significant enough that the child will have much less contact with the other parent, you should weigh this against the potential benefits the move may provide. Relocations cause not only emotional upheavals, but they can create financial difficulties as well, not to mention the psychological impact of essentially removing one parent from the child's life.

Quotes from Children About Living Far from One Parent

"I live with someone I know, and I visit with someone I don't know."

"How do you love someone you've never gotten a chance to know?"

"You love him because he's your dad, but you can't love him for who he is because you don't know him that way."

"I think she was trying to get as far away from Dad as she could."

26

Getting On With Your Life

BY THE TIME YOUR DIVORCE IS FINAL, you will probably disengage emotionally from your ex-spouse and may be anxious to move on. No matter how happy or sad you are to be done with the marriage, you once stood before this person and vowed, "til death do us part." You need to grieve for the loss of your relationship and heal your emotional wounds to begin the next chapter of your life.

Many churches, nonprofit social service agencies and private therapy practices host divorce recovery groups, where divorced people meet on a weekly basis to talk about what they are going through. "Talking about it helps you work through your feelings," says Dr. Maryanne Watson. "After a while, your friends and family may get tired of listening to your pain. The people you meet in divorce recovery groups are going through the same things you are, and with them you can talk about your divorce trauma over and over, as long as you need."

In many divorce recovery groups, you can do more than swap stories. You can also learn how others have dealt with the difficult situations you face, such as problems with children and financial matters. If you join during the divorce, you may hear about the process and procedures you can expect from other members who have already finalized their divorces. Always consult your attorney before acting on any legal advice you receive from others, but talking about and learning from others' mistakes may lessen yours.

Many groups are non-denominational even if a local church is the sponsor or provides the facilities. Your attorney may be able to refer you to one or you can do a search on the internet for listings of groups in your area. Most groups ask for a small donation, but for people without resources, there are free groups.

Dr. Watson advises newly divorced people to wait from one to three years before committing to a new relationship. "If you immediately enter into another relationship, it's easy to make bad decisions when choosing your next partner," she says. "A new relationship is often an attempt to avoid the pain of grief work. Even if you wanted the divorce, you must grieve. If you work through the pain first, your next relationship will be healthier."

Individual counseling can also help you work through your feelings. One therapeutic technique is to write letters to your ex saying all the things you wish you could say in person. Get all of your anger and frustration out, then shred the letters. Even though you won't send them, just the act of writing them can help.

If you have children, the most important thing is not to talk negatively about your ex in front of them. "Your children have a different relationship with your ex than you do," says Dr. Watson. "It's important not to interfere with that."

The Second Time Around

Many people who divorce eventually find new relationships and remarry. According to Dr. Watson, "The number one cause of divorce in couples who remarry is the children from the prior marriages, because the lifecycle of the new family is out of sync with the developmental cycle of the children from the previous relationship. This is especially true of people with teenagers. It's best to remarry after the teens have moved out since teens are trying to detach, while the new blended family is trying to come together."

Dr. Watson advises that if you decide to get married anyway, following two simple rules will help to ease the transition:

1. The biological parent is solely in charge of the children for the first two years; and,
2. The stepparent's job is to be a friend to the children and support the biological parent in his or her discipline.

The goal of these rules is for the relationship with the children to become strong enough for the stepparent to assume the role of a functional parent. The lessons you learned in your divorce can help you be more successful the next time around.

Here are some financial lessons to keep in mind next time:

- Consider some kind of premarital agreement that spells out the financial rules between you simply and clearly.
- Keep financial records, even if your new spouse keeps them too.
- Thoroughly review income tax forms, contracts and other financial instruments before signing them.
- Periodically examine a copy of your credit report.
- Understand the differences between separate and community property and manage them accordingly.

Prenups and Postnups

If you decide to remarry, you may want to have your attorney draft a premarital agreement (*prenup*), especially if you had difficulty dividing assets during your divorce. A prenup is simply a financial contract between two people, signed before marriage, that may confirm or modify the characterization of property in the event of divorce, separation or death.

Prenups can protect assets like retirement accounts, future earnings and income from separate property. They tend to simplify financial situations that can become complicated and messy during a divorce. A premarital agreement cannot be written to adversely affect the rights of any children in need of support in the event of a divorce.

Postmarital agreements (*postnups*) are much like prenups, except you create them after the marriage. Like premarital agreements, postnups must be in writing and signed by both spouses. The postmarital agreement should also specify that you intend to actually partition and exchange property. Through the use of a postnup, spouses may convert community property or separate property into the other spouse's separate property. This way, in the event of a divorce, the property is already divided.

If your new spouse asks you to sign a prenup or postnup, you should be aware that these agreements are difficult to break. Texas law presumes that these financial contracts are enforceable, and therefore the burden of proof to invalidate the agreement is on the person who tries to break it. Since well-written prenups are difficult to overturn, it is important that you understand and agree with the contents of the agreement before you sign it rather than hoping you can tackle its validity later.

Strive for a Successful Divorce

Divorce is not a subject you read about for pleasure. We realize that you are reading these words now because you are either going through the process, are contemplating divorce or know someone close to you who is in the midst of a divorce. Once you or your loved one completes the process, you may have no more use for this book, although the odds are that you will know someone else who is going through a divorce.

Most people read these books in a way that "scratches the itch" that bothers them at that particular moment. You are probably doing the same, hunting through the table of contents for solutions to the problems you are facing at this time. But if you read this book from cover to cover, we believe you are now better equipped with the necessary family law information, whether you get a divorce or plan to stay married the rest of your life.

Understand that even though you, a family member or friend may have suffered a fair amount of emotional and financial heartbreak, you shouldn't let a divorce cast a shadow over your future. Everyone makes mistakes and many of us are unlucky in love. Armed with a toolbox of family law wisdom gained from this experience, we urge you to pursue the next chapter of your life with eyes wide open, with determination and passion.

Lone Star Divorce Bibliography

1. Texas Department of State Health Services. Marriages and Divorces by County, Texas, 2004. (Vital Statistics, Table 39). Retrieved July 6, 2007, from http://www.dshs.state.tx.us/CHS/VSTAT/latest/t39. shtm

2. National Center for Health Statistics. Births, Marriages, Divorces, and Deaths: Provisional Data for 2005. (National Vital Statistics Report, Vol. 54, No. 20, July 21, 2006). Retrieved July 6, 2007, from http://www.cdc.gov/nchs/data/nvsr/nvsr54/nvsr54_20.pdf

3. Texas Department of State Health Services. Marriages & Divorces, Texas, 1975-2004. (Vital Statistics, Table 7). Retrieved July 6, 2007, from http://www.dshs.state.tx.us/chs/vstat/vs04/t07.shtm

4. American Bar Association, National Lawyer Population by State. Retrieved July 6, 2007, from http://www.abanet.org/market-research/2006_national%20_lawyer_population_survey.pdf

5. State Bar of Texas, State Bar Members: Attorney Statistical Profile (2006-07). Retrieved July 6, 2007, from http://www.texasbar.com/Template.cfm?Section=Research_and_Analysis&Template=/ContentManagement/ContentDisplay.cfm&ContentID=17235

6. Statistics: Living Together (a.k.a. cohabitation, or unmarried partner households). (n.d.). Retrieved July 6, 2007, from http://www.unmarried.org/statistics.html

7. Statistics: More about unmarried different-sex couples. (n.d.). Retrieved July 6, 2007, from http://www.unmarried.org/statistics.html

8. National Center for Health Statistics. Births: Final Data for 2004. (National Vital Statistics Reports, Volume 55, Number 1, September 29, 2006). Retrieved July 6, 2007, from http://www.cdc.gov/nchs/data/nvsr/nvsr55/nvsr55_01.pdf

9. More About Trauma & Recovery: Domestic Violence: More Facts: Women in the U.S. (n.d.) Retrieved July 6, 2007, from http://www.juliancenter.org/more_facts.html

10. More About Trauma & Recovery: Domestic Violence: More Facts: Impact on Children. (n.d.) Retrieved July 6, 2007, from http://www.juliancenter.org/more_facts.html

11. Tannen, Deborah. (1998). The Argument Culture: Moving From Debate to Dialog. New York: Random House.

12. Rosenbloom, Gail. (2007, April 1). A Different Divorce. Star Tribune (Minneapolis, MN). Retrieved June 8, 2007, from Highbeam Research database.

13. State of Texas. (n.d.) Application of Guidelines to Net Resources of $7,500 or Less. Texas Fam. Code Ann. 154.125 (vernon 2007).

14. ACES - The Association for Children for Enforcement of Support (n.d.). Retrieved October 16, 2007, from http://www.childsupport-aces.org/acesstatistics.shtml.

15. Internal Revenue Service. (2006). Selling Your Home. (Publication 523). Retrieved July 6, 2007, from http://www.irs.gov/publications/p523/ar02.html#d0e1939

16. Upshaw, Larry. (1995, May) The Age of Divorce. D Magazine, 65-72.

Texas Professionals List

The following pages contain a list of professionals who focus on helping Texas residents through divorce. This list is a resource for divorcing people attempting to solve problems unique to their situation. Although the people listed here are experienced at divorce situations, neither the authors or the publisher guarantee the service of these providers. We invite you to contact one or more of them, interview them to see if their skills match your needs and make a determination, on your own, whether you want to retain their services.

Austin

Accountants

Janet Hagy
3818 Spicewood Springs Rd
Suite 201
Austin, TX 78759
512-346-3782
www.hagycpa.com

Marcia C. Threadgill
8140 North Mopac Expy
Suite 1-270
Austin, TX 78759-8974
512-794-9596
www.austin-cpas.com

Bankruptcy Attorneys

Leslie Howe
819 1/2 West 11th
Austin, TX 78701
512-472-2888
www.lesliemhowepc.com

Business Valuators

Edward C. Fowler
515 Congress Avenue
Suite 1612
Austin, TX 78701
512-476-8866
www.fowlervalue.com

Certified Divorce Financial Analyst

Mary Ann Osborne
512 East 39th
Austin, TX 78751
512-420-9825

Counselors/Psychologists

Diane Ireson
3660 Stone Ridge Rd
Bldg D102
Austin, TX 78746
512-306-8044

Larry Miller, PhD
4131 Spicewood Springs Rd
Suite K-8
Austin, TX 78759
512-502-1882
www.divorcerecoveryaustin.com

D. Ross Miller, PhD
8140 North Mopac Expy
Westpark II Suite 200
Austin, TX 78759
512-346-2332

Estate Planning Attorneys

Kevin Holcomb
401 Congress Ave
Suite 2200
Austin, TX 78701
512-480-5600
www.gdhm.com

Mark Schreiber
2112 Rio Grande St
Austin, TX 78705
512-477-7543
www.rcsp.com

Patricia T. Barnes
2901-D Bee Caves Rd
Austin, TX 78746
512-328-8355
www.texasprobate.com

Financial Planners/ Wealth Managers

Beth Dickson
4550 Post Oak Place
Suite 118
Houston, TX 77027
713-599-1220
www.equitablesolutions.com

Jan Demetri, CPA
3355 Bee Cave Rd
Suite 612
Austin, TX 78746
512-477-7696

Forensic CPAs

Marcia C. Threadgill
8140 North Mopac Expy
Suite 1-270
Austin, TX 78759-8974
512-794-9596
www.austin-cpas.com

Mortgage Brokers

Bob Goodwin
8800 Business Park Dr
Suite 200
Austin, TX 78759
512-241-3192
www.bobfundstexas.com

Nikki Bryant
2224 Walsh Tarlton
Suite 210
Austin, TX 78746
512-413-1164
www.lakehillslending.com

Private Investigators

Claude Bookout
401 Congress Ave
Suite 1540
Austin, TX 78701
512-687-3490
www.investigateworldwide.com

Real Estate Appraisers

Brad Beal
1717 W. 6th St
Suite 295
Austin, TX 78703
512-477-7059

Real Estate Agents

Connie McGlothlin
3700 Bee Caves Rd, Suite 102
Austin, TX 78746
512-554-3387
www.turnquistpartners.com

Susie Dudley
950 Westbank Drive
Suite 100
Austin, TX 78746
512-327-4800
www.ameliabullock.com

Dallas/Fort Worth

Accountants

Alan H. Levi
3710 Rawlins St
Suite 860
Dallas, TX 75219
214-559-0008
www.allenlevicpa.com

Hunter Nibert
5580 LBJ Freeway
Suite 400
Dallas, TX 75240
972-661-1843
www.traviswolff.com

Martin E. Auerbach
12801 N. Central Expy, Suite 1500
Dallas, TX 75243
972-239-4699
www.aagcpa.com

Vance K. Maultsby, Jr.
12222 Merit Dr
Suite 1180
Dallas, TX 75251
214-739-4737
www.hmpc.com

Bankruptcy Attorneys

Michelle Mendez
13155 Noel Rd, Suite 600
Dallas, TX 75240
214-468-3359
www.hunton.com

Business Valuators

Bill Barnard
5580 LBJ Freeway
Suite 400
Dallas, TX 75240
972-720-5213
www.traviswolff.com

David N. Fuller
5221 N. O'Connor Blvd
Suite 830
Irving, TX 75039
972-831-7907
www.valueinc.com

Douglas K. Fejer
6805 Crestland
Dallas, TX 75252
972-713-9300
doug@dougfejer.com

Philip Courtney Hogan
12700 Preston Rd
Suite 185
Dallas, TX 75230
972-490-1120
www.pchogancpa.com

Gerald A. Keller
Hill Schwartz Spilker
Keller LLC
Heritage Square II
5001 LBJ Freeway
Suite 300
Dallas, TX 75244
214-741-5360
www.hsskgroup.com

Elizabeth Ann Schrupp
6223 Lavendale
Dallas, TX 75230
214-361-9651

Counselors/Psychologists

Benjamin J. Albritton
8411 Preston Rd
Dallas, TX 75225
214-265-1400

Thom Allen
14114 Dallas Pkwy
Suite 260
Dallas,TX 75254
214-498-8466
www.pranadynamics.com

Barry S. Coakley, PhD
2665 Villa Creek
Suite 245
Farmers Branch, TX 75234
972-406-1077
www.goodcoparenting.com

Alexandria H. Doyle, PhD
5949 Sherry Ln
Suite 840
Dallas, TX 75225
214-361-5900

Kevin Karlson, PhD
8411 Preston Rd
Suite 675
Dallas, TX 75225
972-839-2394

Philip Korenman, PhD
4975 Preston Blvd
Plano, TX 75023
972-985-4011

Ray Levy, PhD
17480 Dallas Pkwy
Suite 230
Dallas, TX 75287
972-407-1191
www.drraylevy.com

Mark Otis
2925 LBJ Freeway
Suite 180
Dallas, TX 75234
972-241-0674

Honey A. Sheff, PhD
17480 Dallas Pkwy
Suite 230
Dallas, TX 75287
972-733-0075

Patrick Savage
4235 Cedar Springs Rd
Dallas, TX 752219
214-526-3374
www.parkcitiescounseling.com

Jeffrey C. Siegel, PhD
12810 Hillcrest Road, Suite 217
Dallas, TX 75230
972-960-1472

Linda Solomon
8350 North Central Expy
Suite 1175
Dallas, TX 75206
214-361-8771
www.collabneutral.com

Maryanne Watson, PhD
5172 Village Creek Dr
Suite 101
Plano, TX 75093
972-380-8600
www.maryannewatson.com

John Zervopolous
5440 Harvest Hill Rd
Suite 202
Dallas, TX 75230
972-458-8007

Estate Planners

Alan C. Klein
8333 Douglas Ave, Suite 1200
Dallas, TX 75225-5845
214-369-3889
www.kpllp.com

Edward V. Smith, III
2911 Turtle Creek Blvd
Suite 1010
Dallas, TX 75219
214-528-1590

Larry Flournoy Jr.
740 E. Campbell Rd, Suite 560
Richardson, TX 75081
214-369-0361
www.jhflegal.com

Lawrence M. Wolfish
16475 Dallas Pkwy
Suite 395
Addison, TX 75001
972-248-7448

Michael Kaufman
901 Main St
Suite 6000
Dallas, TX 75202
214-953-5734
www.jw.com

W. Thomas Finley
3232 McKinney Ave
Suite 1400
Dallas, TX 75204-2429
214-740-1431
www.bellnunnally.com

*Financial Planners/
Wealth Managers*

Chris Sheppard
Frost Bank
4200 S. Hulen
Ft. Worth, TX 76109
817-420-5064

Christopher Holtby
8117 Preston Rd
Suite 300 West
Dallas, TX 75225
214-706-9053
www.midlandasset.com

Dave Patterson
12750 Merit Dr
Suite 900
Dallas, TX 75251
972-383-8308
www.hfg-dallas.com

Dodee Crockett
5910 N. Central Expwy
Suite 2000
Dallas, TX 75206
214-750-2107

Eric Bennett
5500 Preston Rd
Suite 250
Dallas, TX 75205
214-252-3263
www.tollesonwealth.com

Greg Hall
5500 Preston Rd
Dallas, TX 75205
214-252-3266

Kevin W. Margolis
5310 Harvest Hill, Suite 226
Dallas, TX 75230
972-960-6460
www.sfmgadvisors.com

Mike Jarvis
12377 Merit Dr, Suite 1500
Dallas, TX 75251
972-455-9060
www.mikejarvis.com

Kalita McCarthy
8235 Douglas Ave
Suite 500
Dallas, TX 75225
214-691-6090

Nancy T. Mello
13355 Noel Rd
Suite 700, Floor 07
Dallas, TX 75240
972-896-2131
www.fa.ml.com/nancy_mello

Todd Amacher
5950 Sherry Ln, Suite 500
Dallas, TX 75225
214-360-7000
www.rgtnet.com

Vickie Wise
5956 Sherry Ln, Suite 100
Dallas, TX 75225
214-346-3940
vwise@bokf.com

Forensic CPAs

Douglas K. Fejer
6805 Crestland
Dallas, TX 75252
972-713-9300

Elizabeth Ann Schrupp
6223 Lavendale
Dallas, TX 75230
214-361-9651

Jim Wingate
10440 N. Central Expwy
Suite 610
Dallas, TX 75231
214-750-0640

Vance K. Maultsby Jr.
12222 Merit Dr
Suite 1180
Dallas, TX 75251
214-739-4737
www.hmpc.com

Mortgage Brokers

Mike Wolfe
5800 W. Plano Pkwy
Suite 105
Plano, TX 75093
972-588-9450
www.willowbendmortgage.com

Private Investigators

Duane Krueger
4403 North Central Expy
Suite 1000
Dallas, TX 75205
214-599-9494

Tom Nelson
P.O. Box 260
Allen, TX 75013
972-390-2109

Real Estate Appraisers

Jim Goodrich
2570 Eldorado Pkwy
Suite 110
McKinney, TX 75070
972-529-2828
www.goodrichappraisal.com

Marquett Brewster
25 Highland Park Village
Suite 100-430
Dallas, TX 75205
800-701-6875
www.marquettbrewster.com

Real Estate Appraisers

D.W. Skelton
5924 Royal Ln
Suite 208
Dallas, TX 75230
214-265-1037

Real Estate Agents

Jan Richey
4783 Preston Rd
Suite 100
Frisco, TX 75034
972-712-9898
www.janrichey.com

Kim Salisbury
5823 Brushy Creek Trail
Dallas, TX 75252
214-558-7295

Penny Bradshaw
1201 W Green Oaks Blvd
Arlington, TX 76013
817-654-3737
www.ebby.com

Saundra Stephens-
Woodmansee
6400 West Plano Pkwy
Suite 112
Plano, TX 75093
214-520-4424
www.ebby.com

Retirement/Employment Benefits Attorney

William C. Clifton
8080 N. Central Expwy
Suite 860
Dallas, TX 75206
214-891-7014
wcclifton@msn.com

Tax Attorneys

Charles Billings
14901 Quorum
Suite 740
Dallas, TX 75254
972-387-2513

Houston

Accountants

Geoffrey Poll
1800 Bering Dr
Suite 950
Houston, TX 77057
713-783-5200
www.fcpcpa.com

Business Valuators/ Forensic CPAs

Haran Levy
12 East Greenway Pl, Suite 800
Houston, TX 77046
713-960-1706
www.uhy-us.com

Jeannie McClure
1225 North Loop West
Suite 1050
Houston, TX 77008
713-622-6000
www.businessvalue.net

Patrice Ferguson
1800 Bering Dr
Suite 950
Houston, TX 77057-3129
713-783-5200
www.fcpcpa.com

Counselors/Psychologists

Karen Gollaher
9100 Southwest Freeway
Suite 152
Houston, TX 77074
713-776-9449

Estate Planning

Bernard (Barney) Jones
713-621-3330
www.bejlaw.com

Scott A. Schepps
1360 Post Oak Blvd
Suite 1600
Houston, TX 77056
713-840-7710
www.fizerbeck.com

Financial Planners/ Wealth Managers

Beth Dickson
4550 Post Oak Pl
Suite 118
Houston, TX 77027
713-599-1220
www.equitablesolutions.com

Jeff Swantkowski
5847 San Felipe
Suite 200
Houston, TX 77057
713-344-9302
www.patriotwealth.com

Private Investigators

Robert Grieve
4900 Woodway Dr, Suite 550
Houston, TX 77056
713-963-9916
www.robertgrieve.com

San Antonio

Accountants

Gerald L. Hill
8620 N. New Braunfels
Suite 300
San Antonio, TX 78217
210-340-8351
www.hf-cpa.com

Kimberly C. Ford
8621 N. New Braunfels
Suite 301
San Antonio, TX 78218
210-340-8351
www.hf-cpa.com

Bankruptcy Attorneys

William R. Davis, Jr.
745 East Mulberry
Suite 900
San Antonio, TX 78212
210-736-6600
www.langleybanack.com

Business Valuators/ Forensic CPAs

Gerald L. Hill
8620 N. New Braunfels
Suite 300
San Antonio, TX 78217
210-340-8351
www.hf-cpa.com

Counselors/Psychologists

Robin B. Walton
408 Dwyer
San Antonio, TX 78204
210-223-0779
www.robinbrownwalton.com

Dina Trevino, PhD
7272 Wurzbach, Suite 1504
San Antonio, TX 78240
210-647-7712

Joann Murphey, PhD
1202 West Bitters, Building 3
San Antonio, TX 78216-7739
210-495-0221
www.drjmurphey.com

Private Investigators

Gary Barnes
P.O. Box 6314
San Antonio, TX 78209
210-824-6300
www.barnesinvestigations.com

Real Estate Agents

Tricia Curbello
Century 21
2900 Moss Rock
San Antonio, TX 78230
210-861-1197
www.texasrealestatelady.com

Tyler

Bankruptcy Attorneys

Michael J. McNally
400 First Place
Tyler, TX 75710-1080
903-597-6301
www.mcnallyandpatrick.com

Business Valuators

Robert Bailes
131357 Dominion Plaza
Tyler, TX 75703
903-561-5859
www.bailesco.com

William (Rusty) Bundy
3310 S Broadway Ave
Suite 100
Tyler, TX 75701
903-597-6311
www.henrypeters.com

Marion Shilling
3305 Fry Ave
Tyler, TX 75703
903-593-4717

Counselors/Psychologists

Gayle Burress, PhD
1405 South Fleischel Ave
Suite 332
Tyler, TX 75707
903-592-5455

Robert Sperry
615 Chase Drive, Suite 201
Tyler, TX 75701
903-534-5968
www.drbobsperry.com

Estate Planning Attorneys

John Berry
100 Independence Pl
Suite 400
Tyler, TX 75703
903-561-4200

Mark Boon
1800 N .W. Loop 281
Suite 310
Longview, TX 75604
903-759-2200
www.boonlaw.com

Michael D. Allen
3805 Old Bullard Rd
Tyler, TX 75701
903-534-0006
www.allenlottmann.com

Financial Planners/ Wealth Managers

Ken Dun
6101 S Broadway, Suite 510
Tyler, TX 75703
903-534-4000
www.ubs.com

Private Investigators

Paul Black
903-596-8840
Toll free 877-800-8840
www.lonestarlegalservices.com

Appendix A

Glossary of Family Law Terms

Following are the definitions of many legal terms and other words and phrases you will find mentioned in this book. Please note that these terms have been described as they pertain to divorce and may have other definitions outside of the family law area.

A

ACTION: A lawsuit or proceeding in a court of law.

AFFIDAVIT: A written statement under oath.

ALIMONY: Periodic payments of support provided by one spouse to the other.

ANNULMENT: The marriage is declared void, as though it never took place.

ANSWER: The written response to a petition or motion.

APPEAL: A legal action where parties request that a higher court review the decisions made by the trial court.

ASSET: Anything of value owned by you or your spouse, including real estate, automobiles, furniture, bank accounts, jewelry, life insurance policies, businesses and retirement plans.

B

BENCH TRIAL: A trial where the judge determines all issues and there is no jury.

BILLING: An accounting of hours spent on your case by the attorney, his legal assistant and others. Usually calculated monthly.

BINDING: Placing one or both parties in the divorce under a legal obligation to comply with an agreement or court order. For example, stating that the agreement is binding on both parties means that they are both legally obligated to abide by the agreement, and if they refuse to do so, legal action may be taken against them.

BUSINESS VALUATION: Using experts to determine the value of a business in a divorce context, for the purpose of dividing and awarding assets. The valuation of a closely held business or professional practice is only as good as the judgment of the appraiser and the accuracy of the information relied upon. When valuing a closely held business, it is essential for the appraiser to have a thorough knowledge of the measures of value, the methods of valuation and Texas case law on valuations in the context of a divorce. There may be a need for adjustments to the value of a business interest due to its lack of marketability, the lack of control of a minority interest and the existence of a covenant not to compete.

C

CHARACTERIZATION: The process of identifying what property is separate property and what property is community property. The court can only divide the parties' community property and not their separate property.

CHILD SUPPORT: Money paid from one parent to the other on a regular basis, usually monthly, for the benefit of their minor children.

CLOSELY HELD BUSINESS: A business that is privately owned, such as a family business.

CLOSING ARGUMENTS: Final statements by each attorney at the end of a trial or hearing to summarize to the judge or jury the evidence and the law.

COLLABORATIVE LAW: A process whereby the parties agree to attempt settlement of a divorce outside the court system, in a series of sessions that include the parties, their attorneys and, in some cases, other professional experts.

COMMINGLING ASSETS: When separate and community funds are mixed together, such as in the same bank accounts.

COMMON LAW MARRIAGE: When a man and woman who are free to marry agree to be married, live together as husband and wife and represent to others that they are married, but do not have a formal ceremony with a marriage license.

COMMUNITY DEBTS: All debts incurred during the marriage are presumed to be community debts. This presumption can be rebutted, however, by proving that the creditor agreed to look solely to the separate estate of the spouse who incurred the debt for payment of the debt, and proving that spouse's separate funds were used to repay the debt.

COMMUNITY PROPERTY: Property acquired during the marriage, other than property established by clear and convincing evidence to be separate property is community property and each spouse is entitled to an equitable share upon divorce.

CONTEMPT: Failure to follow a court order. One side can request that the court hold the other side in contempt and punish him or her for violating a court order.

CONTESTED ISSUES: All issues upon which the parties are unable to agree and which the judge or jury must resolve at a hearing or trial.

CONTINGENT ASSET: An asset that you may or may not receive later, such as a recovery from a lawsuit or a potential claim against a third party.

CONTINGENT LIABILITY: A liability that you may or may not owe later, such as a lawsuit against either party or a guaranty that you have signed.

CONTINUANCE: Postponement of a trial or hearing.

CORROBORATING WITNESS: A person who testifies for you and backs up your story.

COUNTERCLAIM: A written request to the court for legal action, which is filed by a respondent after being served with a petition.

COURT REPORTER: The person who records the testimony and other court proceedings.

CROSS EXAMINATION: Questions asked of witnesses who have been called to testify by the opposing attorney.

CUSTODY (SOLE AND JOINT): Refers to the rights and duties that parents have with respect to their children.

D

DECREE OF DIVORCE: The final document that the judge signs granting the divorce. The divorce decree contains all of the agreements of the parties and orders of the court with respect to all issues in the case, including child custody and possession, child support, alimony and division of the community estate and confirmation of any separate estates.

DEFERRED COMPENSATION: Deferred compensation includes pensions, annuities payable in the future and other forms of deferred income.

DEFINED BENEFIT PLAN: An agreement to pay employees a monthly benefit beginning at retirement based on factors specific to each plan, such as years of service, age and salary.

DEFINED CONTRIBUTION PLAN: An employee participating in a defined contribution plan has an individual account to which generally both the employer and the employee make contributions.

DEPOSITION: Discovery method in which an attorney asks questions of the opposing party or another witness while that person is under oath.

DIRECT EXAMINATION: Questions asked of witnesses who have been called to testify by the attorney asking the questions.

DISCOVERY: A way of getting information from the other side or third parties. Examples are interrogatories (written questions to be answered under oath), requests to produce documents and depositions.

DISSOLUTION: Legally ending a marriage. Same as divorce.

DOCKET: A court's schedule of cases to be heard on a particular day.

E

ENJOINED: Prohibited by the court from doing or failing to continue doing a specific act.

EX PARTE: Communication with the judge by only one party or that party's attorney. In order for a judge to speak with either side, in most cases the other side must be properly notified and have an opportunity to be included in the hearing or conference.

EXPERT WITNESS: A person who is qualified as an expert in a certain area may testify as to his or her opinion regarding the matters in which he or she is qualified. For example, when either spouse's testimony as to the value of a certain asset is disputed, the court may consider a valuation supported by expert opinion. Experts in a family law case may include psychologists, business valuation experts, real estate appraisers, forensic CPA's, and others, such as art and airplane appraisers.

F

FAMILY LAW: The entire area of the law that regulates divorce and custody-related matters.

FAULT: The determination of which party is most responsible for the breakup of the marriage. While Texas is a no-fault state, the determination of fault may be used to influence the division of assets.

FILING: Giving the court clerk your legal papers to be included in the court's file. Fees are charged for the filing of some types of papers.

FORENSIC ACCOUNTANT: A person who prepares an investigation of finances or who traces assets for the purpose of discovering information in a lawsuit and offering testimony in court.

G

GOODWILL: There are two types of goodwill: business and personal. Business goodwill (also called commercial goodwill) is the business's reputation and ability, as an institution, to attract and hold business even with a change in ownership. Personal goodwill (also called professional goodwill) is the reputation and ability associated with the individual professional, not the practice or business as a whole, and therefore cannot be transferred to a buyer. The value of a spouse's personal goodwill is not divisible on divorce and is not to be included in the valuation of the professional's practice.

H

HEARING: A legal proceeding before a judge or associate judge on a motion or request other than the final trial.

I

INFORMAL DISCOVERY: The voluntary and informal exchange of information between the parties through their attorneys, as distinguished from formal discovery such as interrogatories and requests to produce documents.

INJUNCTION: An order from a court prohibiting a person from doing something.

INTERROGATORIES: Written questions submitted to a person requesting information in the divorce, which that person must answer under oath.

INVENTORY AND APPRAISEMENT: A list of detailed information regarding a couple's assets and liabilities, both community and separate.

J

JOINT CUSTODY: A legal status in which both parents share rights and duties concerning their children, although it does not mandate an equal amount of authority or possession time for each parent. There is a presumption in favor of joint custody in Texas courts.

JURISDICTION: The authority of the court to hear a case.

JURY: In Texas, you can request a jury trial in most family law actions, although there are restrictions on what issues may be submitted to a jury and the jury's decisions are not always binding on the court.

L

LIABILITIES: Every debt owed by you or your spouse, including mortgages, business loans, car loans, credit cards and other debts.

LITIGATION: The process of preparing for and going to court.

M

MARKET VALUE: Market value is the most common measure of an item's value. It is defined as the amount a willing buyer who desires to buy but is under no obligation to buy would pay to a willing seller who desires to sell but is under no obligation to sell.

MEDIATOR: A person trained to assist parties in reaching an agreement before going to court. Mediators should not take either party's side or give legal advice to either party. They are only responsible for helping the parties reach an agreement and putting that agreement into writing. In many courts, mediation of family law cases is required before going to court.

MOTION: A request made to the court, other than a petition.

N

NO-FAULT DIVORCE: One party must establish that the marriage has become insupportable because of discord or conflict of personalities that destroys the legitimate ends of the marriage relationship and prevents any reasonable expectation of reconciliation.

O

OBJECTION: Notice to the judge by an attorney of an error in the proceedings and a request for a ruling by the judge.

OBLIGEE: A person to whom money, such as child support or alimony, is owed.

OBLIGOR: A person who is ordered by the court to pay money, such as child support or alimony.

OPENING STATEMENT: A brief summary by an attorney of his client's version of the facts and position on the issues and applicable law, generally at the beginning of the trial or hearing.

ORDER: A written decision signed by a judge and included in the case file, usually following a hearing on a party's motion.

OVERRULED: When an attorney objects to something said or done in the courtroom and the judge disagrees with the objecting attorney.

P

PALIMONY: An award of assets from one companion to another when the two people were not legally married but had some agreement that involved their relationship and property. Palimony is not a recognized legal principle in Texas.

PARENTING CLASS: Teaches parents how to work together, help their children cope with divorce and other family issues. Often ordered by the courts in divorce actions involving children.

PARTY: A person involved in a court case, usually as a petitioner or respondent.

PATERNITY (PARENTAGE) ACTION: A lawsuit used to determine whether a designated individual is the father of a specific child or children.

PETITION: The legal paper that begins a court case when it is filed.

PETITIONER: The person who files the petition, the legal paper that begins a court case.

PLEADINGS: The legal documents filed in a court case which contain the parties' requests.

POSTNUPTIAL (POSTMARITAL) AGREEMENT: A written agreement between spouses created during their marriage to govern division of assets and debts and to provide terms for obligations in the event of divorce. Also called a postnup.

PRENUPTIAL (PREMARITAL) AGREEMENT: A written agreement between two prospective spouses who are planning to marry, which goes into effect as soon as the marriage occurs. Premarital agreements allow persons about to marry to confirm or modify the characterization of property. Also called a prenup.

PRIMARY RESIDENCE: The home in which the children spend most of their time.

PROCESS SERVER: A person authorized to serve legal papers on the person or persons who are being sued or subpoenaed to testify as witnesses.

PRO SE LITIGANT: A person who appears in court without the assistance of a lawyer.

Q

QUALIFIED DOMESTIC RELATIONS ORDER (QDRO): Called a "quadro," the most common use is for the division of retirement benefits upon divorce. The QDRO is an order signed by the judge directed to a retirement plan administrator, which permits a non-employee former spouse to receive his or her share of retirement benefits directly.

R

REQUEST FOR ADMISSIONS: A request for one spouse to admit or deny facts or propositions in the case. Failing to answer a request for admissions in a timely manner results in a deemed confirmation of what was asked.

REQUEST FOR DISCLOSURE: A standard list of questions commonly used for the purposes of gathering information in a divorce. The list includes many factual items such as names and contact information for potential witnesses, including any expert witnesses who may be called to testify.

REQUEST FOR PRODUCTION OF DOCUMENTS: A request for specific documents relevant to the case, which generally includes three to five years of financial records and any other documents anticipated to be used by either side at the trial.

RESPONDENT: The person who is served with a petition for divorce.

RESPONSE: A written reply to a petition or motion.

RETAINER: A lump sum of money that is given to an attorney to begin working on a divorce case.

RULING: A court's decision.

S

SEPARATE PROPERTY: A spouse's separate property consists of property owned or claimed by the spouse before marriage; property acquired by a spouse during marriage by gift or inheritance; and recovery for personal injuries sustained by the spouse during marriage, except for any recovery for loss of earnings during marriage. A court cannot divest a spouse of his or her separate property in dividing the marital estate on divorce. A spouse claiming that disputed property is his or her separate property must prove that the property is separate property by clear and convincing evidence.

SERVICE: Personal service is when a copy of a divorce petition (or other initial pleading) that has been filed with the court is hand delivered by a constable or private process server to the other party. Once the initial pleading is personally served, most subsequent pleadings can be served by less formal methods.

SETTLEMENT AGREEMENT: A document that sets out the agreements between the two parties when compromise is reached in a divorce.

SOLE CUSTODY: When one parent is granted control over the children and the other parent has rights and duties only during their times of possession or visitation (except for the right to access information, which exists at all times).

STANDARD POSSESSION ORDER: The Texas Family Code offers guidelines for the possession of minor children. The schedule provided in the standard possession order is ordered in most divorce cases.

STOCK OPTION: The right to buy a designated stock at any time within a specified period at a predetermined price. Stock options may be vested or unvested.

SUBPOENA: A document served on a person requiring their appearance at a certain time and place to testify and/or produce designated documents.

SUSTAINED: When an attorney objects to something said or done in the courtroom and the judge agrees with the objecting attorney.

T

TEMPORARY HEARING: A hearing before a judge or associate judge in which matters affecting the parties during the pendency of the divorce will be decided, such as possession of children, use of property and support payments.

TEMPORARY INJUNCTION: A temporary court order prohibiting someone from specific acts.

TEMPORARY ORDERS: Decisions by a judge or associate judge on matters affecting the parties during the pendency of the divorce, including use of the marital home, temporary custody and possession of the parties' children, payment of temporary spousal support or child support, payment of interim attorney's fees and preparation by each of the parties of an inventory and appraisement of their property.

TEMPORARY RESTRAINING ORDER: When a divorce suit is filed, the court may, without notice to the other party, grant a temporary restraining order to protect the parties and their children and preserve and protect the parties' property. Such an order may prohibit a party from acts such as threatening the other party or spending money or withdrawing funds except for reasonable and necessary living expenses, business expenses and attorney's fees. The temporary restraining order lasts for up to 14 days, unless an extension is granted and is typically converted within that time into a temporary injunction that is applicable to both parties until the divorce is final.

TEMPORARY SPOUSAL SUPPORT: Once a divorce is filed, if one of the spouses does not have access to funds needed for living expenses while the divorce is pending, the other party may be ordered to make monthly payments to them or otherwise provide them access to the funds. If an agreement cannot be reached between the parties, a temporary hearing can be scheduled for the court to set the amount of temporary support.

TEXAS FAMILY CODE: The part of Texas law that regulates marriage, divorce and child custody-related matters.

TRIAL: The final hearing at which all issues in a contested case are decided.

U

UNCONTESTED DIVORCE: A divorce in which the parties reach agreement on all issues without needing mediation or litigation.

V

VALUATION: The process by which the value of an asset is determined. The judge or jury may consider various types of evidence in determining the value of the parties' property.

VENUE: The location of the court where the case is filed.

Appendix B

Sample Joint Custody Language

The following is an example of the typical language in a joint custody order. Wording similar to this will appear in your decree of divorce. Read through it to learn how each of the parenting rights are outlined and then consult with your attorney to find out how you can modify it to fit your situation:

The Court, having considered the circumstances of the parents and of the children, finds that the following orders are in the best interest of the children.

IT IS ORDERED that John Smith and Mary Smith are appointed parent joint managing conservators of the following children: Tyler Smith and Taylor Smith.

IT IS ORDERED that, at all times, John Smith and Mary Smith, as parent joint managing conservators, shall each have the following rights:

1. the right to receive information from any other conservator of the children concerning the health, education, and welfare of the children;

2. the right to confer with the other parent to the extent possible before making a decision concerning the health, education, and welfare of the children;

3. the right of access to medical, dental, psychological, and educational records of the children;

4. the right to consult with a physician, dentist, or psychologist of the children;

5. the right to consult with school officials concerning the children's welfare and educational status, including school activities;

6. the right to attend school activities;

7. the right to be designated on the children's records as a person to be notified in case of an emergency;

8. the right to consent to medical, dental, and surgical treatment during an emergency involving an immediate danger to the health and safety of the children; and

9. the right to manage the estates of the children to the extent the estates have been created by the parent or the parent's family.

IT IS ORDERED that, at all times, John Smith and Mary Smith, as parent joint managing conservators, shall each have the following duties:

1. the duty to inform the other conservators of the children in a timely manner of significant information concerning the health, education, and welfare of the children; and

2. the duty to inform the other conservators of the children if the conservator resides with for at least thirty days, marries, or intends to marry a person who the conservator knows is registered as a sex offender under chapter 62 of the Code of Criminal Procedure or is currently charged with an offense for which on conviction the person would be required

to register under that chapter. IT IS ORDERED that this information shall be tendered in the form of a notice made as soon as practicable, but not later than the fortieth day after the date the conservator of the children begins to reside with the person or on the tenth day after the date the marriage occurs, as appropriate. IT IS ORDERED that the notice must include a description of the offense that is the basis of the person's requirement to register as a sex offender or of the offense with which the person is charged. WARNING: A CONSERVATOR COMMITS AN OFFENSE PUNISHABLE AS A CLASS C MISDEMEANOR IF THE CONSERVATOR FAILS TO PROVIDE THIS NOTICE.

IT IS ORDERED that, during their respective periods of possession, John Smith and Mary Smith, as parent joint managing conservators, shall each have the following rights and duties:

1. the duty of care, control, protection, and reasonable discipline of the children;

2. the duty to support the children, including providing the children with clothing, food, shelter, and medical and dental care not involving an invasive procedure;

3. the right to consent for the children to medical and dental care not involving an invasive procedure; and

4. the right to direct the moral and religious training of the children.

IT IS ORDERED that John Smith, as a parent joint managing conservator, shall have the following rights and duty:

1. the right, subject to the agreement of the other parent con-

servator, to consent to medical, dental, and surgical treatment involving invasive procedures;

2. the right, subject to the agreement of the other parent conservator, to consent to psychiatric and psychological treatment of the children;

3. the right, subject to the agreement of the other parent conservator, to represent the children in legal action and to make other decisions of substantial legal significance concerning the children;

4. the right, subject to the agreement of the other parent conservator, to consent to marriage and to enlistment in the armed forces of the United States;

5. the right, subject to the agreement of the other parent conservator, to make decisions concerning the children's education;

6. except as provided by section 264.0111 of the Texas Family Code, the right, subject to the agreement of the other parent conservator, to the services and earnings of the children;

7. except when a guardian of the children's estates or a guardian or attorney ad litem has been appointed for the children, the right, subject to the agreement of the other parent conservator, to act as an agent of the children in relation to the children's estates if the children's action is required by a state, the United States, or a foreign government; and

8. the duty, subject to the agreement of the other parent conservator, to manage the estates of the children to the extent the estates have been created by community property or the joint property of the parents.

IT IS ORDERED that Mary Smith, as a parent joint managing conservator, shall have the following rights and duty:

1. the exclusive right to designate the primary residence of the children within Dallas County, Texas;

2. the right, subject to the agreement of the other parent conservator, to consent to medical, dental, and surgical treatment involving invasive procedures;

3. the right, subject to the agreement of the other parent conservator, to consent to psychiatric and psychological treatment of the children;

4. the exclusive right to receive and give receipt for periodic payments for the support of the children and to hold or disburse these funds for the benefit of the children;

5. the right, subject to the agreement of the other parent conservator, to represent the children in legal action and to make other decisions of substantial legal significance concerning the children;

6. the right, subject to the agreement of the other parent conservator, to consent to marriage and to enlistment in the armed forces of the United States;

7. the right, subject to the agreement of the other parent conservator, to make decisions concerning the children's education;

8. except as provided by section 264.0111 of the Texas Family Code, the right, subject to the agreement of the other parent conservator, to the services and earnings of the children;

9. except when a guardian of the children's estates or a guardian or attorney ad litem has been appointed for the children, the right, subject to the agreement of the other parent conservator, to act as an agent of the children in relation to the children's estates if the children's action is required by a state, the United States, or a foreign government; and

10. the duty, subject to the agreement of the other parent conservator, to manage the estates of the children to the extent the estates have been created by community property or the joint property of the parents.

The Court finds that, in accordance with section 153.001 of the Texas Family Code, it is the public policy of Texas to assure that children will have frequent and continuing contact with parents who have shown the ability to act in the best interest of the children, to provide a safe, stable, and nonviolent environment for the children, and to encourage parents to share in the rights and duties of raising their children after the parents have separated or dissolved their marriage. IT IS ORDERED that the primary residence of the children shall be Dallas County, Texas, and the parties shall not remove the children from Dallas County, Texas, for the purpose of changing the primary residence of the children until modified by further order of the court of continuing jurisdiction or by written agreement signed by the parties and filed with the court. IT IS FURTHER ORDERED that Mary Smith shall have the exclusive right to designate the children's primary residence within Dallas County, Texas. IT IS ORDERED that this geographical restriction on the residence of the children shall be lifted if, at the time Mary Smith wishes to remove the children from Dallas County, Texas for the purpose of changing the primary residence of the children, John Smith does not reside in Dallas County, Texas.

Appendix C

Standard Possession Order

Following is the typical form language known as the standard possession order. It is the most common visitation schedule used by Texas courts. Since joint custody is ordered in most cases rather than sold custody, the terms "sole managing conservator" and "possessory conservator" in the form are normally replaced with the parents' names. Consult with your attorney about modifications you would like to make to this schedule:

The Court finds that the following provisions of this Standard Possession Order are intended to and do comply with the requirements of Texas Family Code sections 153.311 through 153.317. IT IS ORDERED that each conservator shall comply with all terms and conditions of this Standard Possession Order. IT IS ORDERED that this Standard Possession Order is effective immediately and applies to all periods of possession occurring on and after the date the Court signs this Standard Possession Order. IT IS, THEREFORE, ORDERED:

(a) Definitions

1. In this Standard Possession Order Aschool@ means the primary or secondary school in which the child is enrolled or, if the child is not enrolled in a primary or secondary school, the public school district in which the child primarily resides.

2. In this Standard Possession Order Achild@ includes each child, whether one or more, who is a subject of this suit while that child is under the age of eighteen years and not otherwise emancipated.

(b) Mutual Agreement or Specified Terms for Possession

IT IS ORDERED that the conservators shall have possession of the child at times mutually agreed to in advance by the parties, and, in the absence of mutual agreement, it is ORDERED that the conservators shall have possession of the child under the specified terms set out in this Standard Possession Order.

(c) Parents Who Reside 100 Miles or Less Apart

Except as otherwise explicitly provided in this Standard Possession Order, when Possessory Conservator resides 100 miles or less from the primary residence of the child, Possessory Conservator shall have the right to possession of the child as follows:

1. Weekends – On weekends, beginning at [select one: 6:00 p.m./the time the child's school is regularly dismissed/or specify other time elected between school dismissal and 6:00 p.m.], on the first, third, and fifth Friday of each month and ending at [select one: 6:00 p.m. on the following Sunday/the time the child's school resumes after the weekend].

2. Weekend Possession Extended by a Holiday – Except as otherwise explicitly provided in this Standard Possession Order, if a weekend period of possession by Possessory Conservator begins on a Friday that is a school holiday during the regular school term or a federal, state, or local holiday during the summer months when school is not in session, or if the period ends on or is immediately followed by a Monday that is such a holiday, that weekend period of possession shall begin at [select one: 6:00 p.m./the time the child's school is regularly dismissed/or specify other time elected between school dismissal and 6:00 p.m.] on the Thursday immediately preceding the Friday holiday or school holiday or end [select one: at 6:00 p.m. on that Monday holiday or school holiday/at 6:00 p.m. on

that Monday holiday or at the time school resumes after that school holiday], as applicable.

3. Thursdays – On Thursday of each week during the regular school term, beginning at [select one: 6:00 p.m./the time the child's school is regularly dismissed/or specify other time elected between school dismissal and 6:00 p.m.] and ending at [select one: 8:00 p.m./ the time the child's school resumes on Friday].

4. Spring Break in Even-Numbered Years – In even-numbered years, beginning at [select one: 6:00 p.m./the time the child's school is regularly dismissed/or specify other time elected between school dismissal and 6:00 p.m.] on the day the child is dismissed from school for the school's spring vacation and ending at [select one: 6:00 p.m. on the day before/the time] school resumes after that vacation.

5. Extended Summer Possession by Possessory Conservator

With Written Notice by April 1 – If Possessory Conservator gives Sole Managing Conservator written notice by April 1 of a year specifying an extended period or periods of summer possession for that year, Possessory Conservator shall have possession of the child for thirty days beginning no earlier than the day after the child's school is dismissed for the summer vacation and ending no later than seven days before school resumes at the end of the summer vacation in that year, to be exercised in no more than two separate periods of at least seven consecutive days each, as specified in the written notice [include if applicable: , provided that the period or periods of extended summer possession do not interfere with Father's Day Weekend]. These periods of possession shall begin and end at 6:00 p.m.

Without Written Notice by April 1 – If Possessory Conservator does not give Sole Managing Conservator written notice by April 1 of a year specifying an extended period or periods of summer possession for that year, Possessory Conservator shall have possession of the child for thirty consecutive days in that year beginning at 6:00 p.m. on July 1 and ending at 6:00 p.m. on July 31.

Notwithstanding the weekend and Thursday periods of possession ORDERED for Possessory Conservator, it is explicitly ORDERED that Sole Managing Conservator shall have a superior right of possession of the child as follows:

1. Spring Break in Odd-Numbered Years – In odd-numbered years, beginning at 6:00 p.m. on the day the child is dismissed from school for the school's spring vacation and ending at 6:00 p.m. on the day before school resumes after that vacation.

2. Summer Weekend Possession by Sole Managing Conservator – If Sole Managing Conservator gives Possessory Conservator written notice by April 15 of a year, Sole Managing Conservator shall have possession of the child on any one weekend beginning at 6:00 p.m. on Friday and ending at 6:00 p.m. on the following Sunday during any one period of the extended summer possession by Possessory Conservator in that year, provided that Sole Managing Conservator picks up the child from Possessory Conservator and returns the child to that same place [include if applicable: and that the weekend so designated does not interfere with Father's Day Weekend].

3. Extended Summer Possession by Sole Managing Conservator – If Sole Managing Conservator gives Possessory Conservator written notice by April 15 of a year or gives Possessory Conservator fourteen days' written notice on or after April 16 of a year, Sole Managing Conservator may designate one weekend beginning no earlier than the day after the child's school is dismissed for the summer vacation and ending no later than seven days before school

resumes at the end of the summer vacation, during which an otherwise scheduled weekend period of possession by Possessory Conservator shall not take place in that year, provided that the weekend so designated does not interfere with Possessory Conservator's period or periods of extended summer possession [include if applicable: or with Father's Day Weekend].

(d) Parents Who Reside More Than 100 Miles Apart

Except as otherwise explicitly provided in this Standard Possession Order, when Possessory Conservator resides more than 100 miles from the residence of the child, Possessory Conservator shall have the right to possession of the child as follows:

1. Weekends – Unless Possessory Conservator elects the alternative period of weekend possession described in the next paragraph, Possessory Conservator shall have the right to possession of the child on weekends, beginning at [select one: 6:00 p.m./the time the child's school is regularly dismissed/or specify other time elected between school dismissal and 6:00 p.m.], on the first, third, and fifth Friday of each month and ending at [select one: 6:00 p.m. on the following Sunday/the time the child's school resumes after the weekend]. Except as otherwise explicitly provided in this Standard Possession Order, if such a weekend period of possession by Possessory Conservator begins on a Friday that is a school holiday during the regular school term or a federal, state, or local holiday during the summer months when school is not in session, or if the period ends on or is immediately followed by a Monday that is such a holiday, that weekend period of possession shall begin at [select one: 6:00 p.m./the time the child's school is regularly dismissed/or specify other time elected between school dismissal and 6:00 p.m.] on the Thursday immediately preceding the Friday holiday or school holiday or end [select one: at 6:00 p.m. on that Monday holiday or school holiday/at 6:00 p.m. on that Monday holiday or at the time school resumes after that school holiday], as applicable.

Alternate Weekend Possession – In lieu of the weekend possession described in the foregoing paragraph, Possessory Conservator shall have the right to possession of the child not more than one weekend per month of Possessory Conservator's choice beginning at [select one: 6:00 p.m./the time the child's school is regularly dismissed/or specify other time elected between school dismissal and 6:00 p.m.] on the day school recesses for the weekend and ending at [select one: 6:00 p.m. on the day before school resumes/the time the child's school resumes] after the weekend. Except as otherwise explicitly provided in this Standard Possession Order, if such a weekend period of possession by Possessory Conservator begins on a Friday that is a school holiday during the regular school term or a federal, state, or local holiday during the summer months when school is not in session, or if the period ends on or is immediately followed by a Monday that is such a holiday, that weekend period of possession shall begin at [select one: 6:00 p.m./the time the child's school is regularly dismissed/or specify other time elected between school dismissal and 6:00 p.m.] on the Thursday immediately preceding the Friday holiday or school holiday or end [select one: at 6:00 p.m. on that Monday holiday or school holiday/at 6:00 p.m. on that Monday holiday or at the time school resumes after that school holiday], as applicable. Possessory Conservator may elect an option for this alternative period of weekend possession by giving written notice to Sole Managing Conservator within ninety days after the parties begin to reside more than 100 miles apart. If Possessory Conservator makes this election, Possessory Conservator shall give Managing Conservator fourteen days' written or telephonic notice preceding a designated weekend. The weekends chosen shall not conflict with the provisions regarding Christmas, Thanksgiving, the child's birthday, and [Father's/Mother's] Day Weekend below.

1.   Weekends – On weekends, beginning at [select one: 6:00 p.m./the time the child's school is regularly dismissed/or specify other time elected between school dismissal and 6:00 p.m.]

on the first, third, and fifth Friday of each month, and ending at [select one: 6:00 p.m. on the following Sunday/the time the child's school resumes after the weekend]. Except as otherwise explicitly provided in this Standard Possession Order, if a weekend period of possession by Possessory Conservator begins on a Friday that is a school holiday during the regular school term or a federal, state, or local holiday during the summer months when school is not in session, or if the period ends on or is immediately followed by a Monday that is such a holiday, that weekend period of possession shall begin at [select one: 6:00 p.m./the time the child's school is regularly dismissed/or specify other time elected between school dismissal and 6:00 p.m.] on the Thursday immediately preceding the Friday holiday or school holiday or end [select one: at 6:00 p.m. on that Monday holiday or school holiday/at 6:00 p.m. on that Monday holiday or at the time school resumes after that school holiday], as applicable.

1.   Weekend – One weekend per month, of Possessory Conservator's choice, beginning at [select one: 6:00 p.m./the time the child's school is regularly dismissed/or specify other time elected between school dismissal and 6:00 p.m.] on the day school recesses for the weekend and ending at [select one: 6:00 p.m. on the day before school resumes/the time the child's school resumes] after the weekend, provided that Possessory Conservator gives Sole Managing Conservator fourteen days' written or telephonic notice preceding a designated weekend. The weekends chosen shall not conflict with the provisions regarding Christmas, Thanksgiving, the child's birthday, and [Father's/Mother's] Day Weekend below.

2.   Spring Break in All Years – Every year, beginning at [select one: 6:00 p.m./the time the child's school is regularly dismissed/or specify other time elected between school dismissal and 6:00 p.m.] on the day the child is dismissed from school for the school's spring vacation and ending at [select one: 6:00 p.m. on the day before/the time] school resumes after that vacation.

3. Extended Summer Possession by Possessory Conservator

With Written Notice by April 1 – If Possessory Conservator gives Sole Managing Conservator written notice by April 1 of a year specifying an extended period or periods of summer possession for that year, Possessory Conservator shall have possession of the child for forty-two days beginning no earlier than the day after the child's school is dismissed for the summer vacation and ending no later than seven days before school resumes at the end of the summer vacation in that year, to be exercised in no more than two separate periods of at least seven consecutive days each, as specified in the written notice [include if applicable: , provided that the period or periods of extended summer possession do not interfere with Father's Day Weekend]. These periods of possession shall begin and end at 6:00 p.m.

Without Written Notice by April 1 – If Possessory Conservator does not give Sole Managing Conservator written notice by April 1 of a year specifying an extended period or periods of summer possession for that year, Possessory Conservator shall have possession of the child for forty-two consecutive days beginning at 6:00 p.m. on June 15 and ending at 6:00 p.m. on July 27 of that year.

Notwithstanding the weekend periods of possession ORDERED for Possessory Conservator, it is explicitly ORDERED that Sole Managing Conservator shall have a superior right of possession of the child as follows:

1. Summer Weekend Possession by Sole Managing Conservator – If Sole Managing Conservator gives Possessory Conservator written notice by April 15 of a year, Sole Managing Conservator shall have possession of the child on any one weekend beginning at 6:00 p.m. on Friday and ending at 6:00 p.m. on the following Sunday during any one period of possession by Possessory Conservator

during Possessory Conservator's extended summer possession in that year, provided that if a period of possession by Possessory Conservator in that year exceeds thirty days, Sole Managing Conservator may have possession of the child under the terms of this provision on any two nonconsecutive weekends during that period and provided that Sole Managing Conservator picks up the child from Possessory Conservator and returns the child to that same place [include if applicable: and that the weekend so designated does not interfere with Father's Day Weekend].

2. Extended Summer Possession by Sole Managing Conservator – If Sole Managing Conservator gives Possessory Conservator written notice by April 15 of a year, Sole Managing Conservator may designate twenty-one days beginning no earlier than the day after the child's school is dismissed for the summer vacation and ending no later than seven days before school resumes at the end of the summer vacation in that year, to be exercised in no more than two separate periods of at least seven consecutive days each, during which Possessory Conservator shall not have possession of the child, provided that the period or periods so designated do not interfere with Possessory Conservator's period or periods of extended summer possession [include if applicable: or with Father's Day Weekend].

(e) Holidays Unaffected by Distance

Notwithstanding the weekend and Thursday periods of possession of Possessory Conservator, Sole Managing Conservator and Possessory Conservator shall have the right to possession of the child as follows:

1. Christmas Holidays in Even-Numbered Years – In even-numbered years, Possessory Conservator shall have the right to possession of the child beginning at [select one: 6:00 P.M./the time

the child's school is regularly dismissed/or specify other time elected between school dismissal and 6:00 P.M.] on the day the child is dismissed from school for the Christmas school vacation and ending at noon on December 26, and Sole Managing Conservator shall have the right to possession of the child beginning at noon on December 26 and ending at 6:00 P.M. on the day before school resumes after that Christmas school vacation.

2. Christmas Holidays in Odd-Numbered Years – In odd-numbered years, Sole Managing Conservator shall have the right to possession of the child beginning at 6:00 p.m. on the day the child is dismissed from school for the Christmas school vacation and ending at noon on December 26, and Possessory Conservator shall have the right to possession of the child beginning at noon on December 26 and ending at [select one: 6:00 p.m. on the day before/the time] the child's school resumes after that Christmas school vacation.

3. Thanksgiving in Odd-Numbered Years – In odd-numbered years, Possessory Conservator shall have the right to possession of the child beginning at [select one: 6:00 p.m./the time the child's school is regularly dismissed/or specify other time elected between school dismissal and 6:00 p.m.] on the day the child is dismissed from school for the Thanksgiving holiday and ending at [select one: 6:00 p.m. on the Sunday following Thanksgiving/the time the child's school resumes after that Thanksgiving holiday].

4. Thanksgiving in Even-Numbered Years – In even-numbered years, Sole Managing Conservator shall have the right to possession of the child beginning at 6:00 p.m. on the day the child is dismissed from school for the Thanksgiving holiday and ending at 6:00 p.m. on the Sunday following Thanksgiving.

5. Child's Birthday – If a conservator is not otherwise entitled under this Standard Possession Order to present possession of [the/

a] child on the child's birthday, that conservator shall have possession of the child [include if desired: and the child's minor siblings] beginning at 6:00 p.m. and ending at 8:00 p.m. on that day, provided that that conservator picks up the child[ren] from the other conservator's residence and returns the child[ren] to that same place.

6. Father's Day Weekend – Father shall have the right to possession of the child each year, beginning at 6:00 p.m. on the Friday preceding Father's Day and ending at 6:00 p.m. on Father's Day, provided that if Father is not otherwise entitled under this Standard Possession Order to present possession of the child, he shall pick up the child from the other conservator's residence and return the child to that same place.

7. Mother's Day Weekend – Mother shall have the right to possession of the child each year, beginning at 6:00 p.m. on the Friday preceding Mother's Day and ending at 6:00 p.m. on Mother's Day, provided that if Mother is not otherwise entitled under this Standard Possession Order to present possession of the child, she shall pick up the child from the other conservator's residence and return the child to that same place.

(f) Undesignated Periods of Possession

Sole Managing Conservator shall have the right of possession of the child at all other times not specifically designated in this Standard Possession Order for Possessory Conservator.

(g) General Terms and Conditions

Except as otherwise explicitly provided in this Standard Possession Order, the terms and conditions of possession of the child that apply regardless of the distance between the residence of a parent and the child are as follows:

1.   Surrender of Child by Sole Managing Conservator – Sole Managing Conservator is ORDERED to surrender the child to Possessory Conservator at the beginning of each period of Possessory Conservator's possession at the residence of Sole Managing Conservator.

If a period of possession by Possessory Conservator begins at the time the child's school is regularly dismissed, Sole Managing Conservator is ORDERED to surrender the child to Possessory Conservator at the beginning of each such period of possession at the school in which the child is enrolled. If the child is not in school, Possessory Conservator shall pick up the child at the residence of Sole Managing Conservator at [time], and Sole Managing Conservator is ORDERED to surrender the child to Possessory Conservator at the residence of Sole Managing Conservator at [time] under these circumstances.

[select one of the following:]

2. Surrender of Child by Possessory Conservator – Possessory Conservator is ORDERED to surrender the child to Sole Managing Conservator at the residence of Possessory Conservator at the end of each period of possession.

2. Return of Child by Possessory Conservator – Possessory Conservator is ORDERED to return the child to the residence of Sole Managing Conservator at the end of each period of possession. However, it is ORDERED that, if Sole Managing Conservator and Possessory Conservator live in the same county at the time of rendition of this order, Possessory Conservator's county of residence remains the same after rendition of this order, and Sole Managing Conservator's county of residence changes, effective on the date of the change of residence by Sole Managing Conservator, Possessory Conservator shall surrender the child to Sole Managing Conserva-

tor at the residence of Possessory Conservator at the end of each period of possession.

If a period of possession by Possessory Conservator ends at the time the child's school resumes, Possessory Conservator is ORDERED to surrender the child to Sole Managing Conservator at the end of each such period of possession at the school in which the child is enrolled or, if the child is not in school, at the residence of Sole Managing Conservator at [time].

3. Surrender of Child by Possessory Conservator – Possessory Conservator is ORDERED to surrender the child to Sole Managing Conservator, if the child is in Possessory Conservator's possession or subject to Possessory Conservator's control, at the beginning of each period of Sole Managing Conservator's exclusive periods of possession, at the place designated in this Standard Possession Order.

4. Return of Child by Sole Managing Conservator – Sole Managing Conservator is ORDERED to return the child to Possessory Conservator, if Possessory Conservator is entitled to possession of the child, at the end of each of Sole Managing Conservator's exclusive periods of possession, at the place designated in this Standard Possession Order.

5. Personal Effects – Each conservator is ORDERED to return with the child the personal effects that the child brought at the beginning of the period of possession.

6. Designation of Competent Adult – Each conservator may designate any competent adult to pick up and return the child, as applicable. IT IS ORDERED that a conservator or a designated competent adult be present when the child is picked up or returned.

7. Inability to Exercise Possession – Each conservator is ORDERED to give notice to the person in possession of the child on each occasion that the conservator will be unable to exercise that conservator's right of possession for any specified period.

8. Written Notice – Written notice shall be deemed to have been timely made if received or postmarked before or at the time that notice is due.

9. Notice to School and Sole Managing Conservator – If Possessory Conservator's time of possession of the child ends at the time school resumes and for any reason the child is not or will not be returned to school, Possessory Conservator shall immediately notify the school and Sole Managing Conservator that the child will not be or has not been returned to school.

This concludes the Standard Possession Order.

Appendix D

Post-Divorce Checklist

Checklist Items	Needs to be done	Completed
Consider an appeal, discuss with attorney		
Update your will		
Update general power of attorney		
Update medical power of attorney		
Update medical directive		
Prepare, record property deeds		
Transfer automobile titles		
Change automobile insurance		
Forward QDRO to plan administrator		
Life insurance – notify carrier of beneficiary change		
Health insurance – notify carrier, order new ID cards		
Update bank accounts		
Update safety deposit box		
Taxes – IRS forms		
Sign IRS Form 8332 (dependency exemption) if ordered		
Update Form W-4		

Checklist Items	Needs to be done	Completed
Update retirement accounts/IRA/pension		
Income withholding orders – request court to deliver		
For women changing back to maiden name, request name change for driver's license, social security card, passport		
Inform creditors of name, address change		
Change name, address on bank accounts		
Notify all others of name, address change		
Other		

Appendix E

IRS Form 8332
Dependency Exemption

<table>
<tr><td>Form 8332
(Rev. January 2006)
Department of the Treasury
Internal Revenue Service</td><td align="center">Release of Claim to Exemption
for Child of Divorced or Separated Parents
► Attach to noncustodial parent's return each year exemption is claimed.</td><td>OMB No. 1545-0074

Attachment
Sequence No. 115</td></tr>
</table>

Name of noncustodial parent claiming exemption	Noncustodial parent's social security number (SSN) ►

Part I   Release of Claim to Exemption for Current Year

I agree not to claim an exemption for _____
                                                        Name(s) of child (or children)

for the tax year 20 _____ .

Signature of custodial parent releasing claim to exemption	Custodial parent's SSN	Date

Note. If you choose not to claim an exemption for this child (or children) for future tax years, also complete Part II.

Part II   Release of Claim to Exemption for Future Years (If completed, see **Noncustodial parent** on page 2.)

I agree not to claim an exemption for _____
                                                        Name(s) of child (or children)

for the tax year(s) _____ .
                (Specify. See instructions.)

Signature of custodial parent releasing claim to exemption	Custodial parent's SSN	Date

General Instructions

Purpose of form. If you are a custodial parent, you can use this form to release your claim to a dependency exemption for your child. The release of the dependency exemption will also release to the noncustodial parent the child tax credit and the additional child tax credit (if either applies). Complete this form (or a similar statement containing the same information required by this form) and give it to the noncustodial parent who will claim the child's exemption. The noncustodial parent must attach this form or a similar statement to his or her tax return each year the exemption is claimed.

You are the custodial parent if you had custody of the child for the greater part of the year. You are the noncustodial parent if you had custody for a shorter period of time or did not have custody at all.

Exemption for a dependent child. A dependent is either a qualifying child or a qualifying relative. In most cases, a child of divorced or separated parents will qualify as a dependent of the custodial parent under the rules for a qualifying child. However, the noncustodial parent may be able to claim the child's exemption if the *Special rule for children of divorced or separated parents* on this page applies.

For the definition of a qualifying child and a qualifying relative, see your tax return instruction booklet.

Post-1984 decree or agreement. If the divorce decree or separation agreement went into effect after 1984, the noncustodial parent can attach certain pages from the decree or agreement instead of Form 8332. To be able to do this, the decree or agreement must state all three of the following.

1. The noncustodial parent can claim the child as a dependent without regard to any condition (such as payment of support).

2. The other parent will not claim the child as a dependent.

3. The years for which the claim is released.

The noncustodial parent must attach all of the following pages from the decree or agreement.

• Cover page (include the other parent's SSN on that page).

• The pages that include all of the information identified in (1) through (3) above.

• Signature page with the other parent's signature and date of agreement.

 The noncustodial parent must attach the required information even if it was filed with a return in an earlier year.

Special rule for children of divorced or separated parents. A child is treated as a qualifying child or a qualifying relative of the noncustodial parent if all of the following apply.

1. The child received over half of his or her support for the year from one or both of the parents (see the *Exception* on this page). Public assistance payments, such as Temporary Assistance for Needy Families (TANF), are not support provided by the parents.

2. The child was in the custody of one or both of the parents for more than half of the year.

3. Either of the following applies.

a. The custodial parent agrees not to claim the child's exemption by signing this form or a similar statement. If the decree or agreement went into effect after 1984, see *Post-1984 decree or agreement* on this page.

b. A pre-1985 decree of divorce or separate maintenance or written separation agreement states that the noncustodial parent can claim the child as a dependent. But the noncustodial parent must provide at least $600 for the child's support during the year. This rule does not apply if the decree or agreement was changed after 1984 to say that the noncustodial parent cannot claim the child as a dependent.

For this rule to apply, the parents must be one of the following.

• Divorced or legally separated under a decree of divorce or separate maintenance.

• Separated under a written separation agreement.

• Living apart at all times during the last 6 months of the year.

If this rule applies, and the other dependency tests in your tax return instruction booklet are also met, the noncustodial parent can claim the child's exemption.

Exception. If the support of the child is determined under a multiple support agreement, this special rule does not apply and this form should not be used.

For Paperwork Reduction Act Notice, see back of form.   Cat. No. 13910F   Form **8332** (Rev. 1-2006)

Texas Divorce Resources

Domestic Violence

National Domestic Violence Hotline
800-799-SAFE
www.ndvh.org
Hotline open 24 hours a day, 365 days a year, providing crisis intervention, safety planning, information and referrals. Assistance is available in English and Spanish.

National Sexual Assault Hotline
800-656-HOPE
www.rainn.org
Call or go online for crisis intervention, support and referrals to a local crisis center. Also has online live chat that works like instant messaging, and is free and confidential.

Texas Council on Family Violence
www.tcfv.org
To find programs and shelters in Texas near you, go to Quick Links down the left side of their website, and click on Service Directory. There you can search by city, county or program.

State of Texas Services & Organizations

Texas Attorney General's Office
800-252-8011 Public Information & Assistance
512-460-6000 Child Support State Office
800-252-8014 Automated Payment and Case Information

www.oag.state.tx.us
Call or visit their website for information about child support.

State Bar of Texas
800-204-2222
www.texasbar.com
Click on "Additional Information for the Public" for help and questions about finding an attorney. They also offer pamphlets on various family law issues.

Texas Department of Family and Protective Services
800-252-5400 to report child abuse or neglect
www.dfps.state.tx.us

Child Support Information

Attorney General of Texas – Child Support Division
512-460-6000 Child Support State Office
800-252-8014 Automated Payment and Case Information
www.oag.state.tx.us/cs/

Child Support Interactive
For payment, case status and other basic services regarding child support.
800-252-8014
http://childsupport.oag.state.tx.us

ACES – Association for Children for Enforcement of Support
214-553-5935
www.acestexas.org
Non-profit organization helping to educate parents about their rights and working to improve child support enforcement.

Collaborative Law

Collaborative Law Institute of Texas
972-386-0158
www.collablawtexas.com
Find out more about collaborative law through articles and FAQ's, and click on the map to find a collaborative professional near you.

International Academy of Collaborative Professionals
www.collaborativepractice.com
Their "For the Public" section contains lots of helpful information. Don't miss the Links section, which lists websites that deal with all aspects and issues of divorce.

Children & Parenting

Kid's Turn
www.kidsturn.org
A site to help kids learn about divorce. Includes games, articles and activities, as well as a listing of children's books about divorce.

Child & Family Guidance Center
214-351-3490
www.childrenandfamilies.org
Non-profit mental health agency serving children and adults in the Dallas area.

Child Abuse Prevention Center
214-370-9810
www.excap.org
Provider of prevention services for at-risk children in Dallas county.

Children in the Middle
972-897-0440
www.childreninthemiddle.com
Site is designed to support adults in raising children between two homes. Conducts parenting classes in the Dallas and Houston areas.

For Kids' Sake
512-476-9490
www.for-kids-sake.com
Austin based organization that helps people learn how to parent more effectively.

Children's Rights Council
www.crckids.org
Dedicated to assisting children of separation and divorce through advocacy and parental education.

Divorce Websites

Divorce Online
www.divorceonline.com
Numerous articles on the financial, legal and psychological aspects of divorce.

DivorceNet
www.divorcenet.com
Largest divorce resource online, with articles, forums, and search features to find divorce-related professionals in your area.

Divorce Central
www.divorcecentral.com
Lots of information and resources, including a section on parenting during divorce.

Divorce Recovery Groups

Many churches and other organizations host non-denominational divorce recovery groups. If you're not sure how to find a local group, check out these online listings to search for one in your area.

Divorce Source
www.divorcesource.com/groups/texas.shtml

Divorce Magazine
www.divorcemag.com/TX/support/index.shtml

Divorce Care
www.divorcecare.com

Divorce Headquarters
www.divorcehq.com/spprtgroups.shtml

Other Support Organizations

Grandparents Raising Grandchildren
www.raisingyourgrandchildren.com
Site contains resources and information for those raising grandchildren.

Texas Fathers for Equal Rights
817-457-DADS (3237)
www.tferfw.org/tfer/
Dedicated to educating people about their rights in family courts.

Fathers.com
www.fathers.com
Website for the National Center for Fathering. Offers tips and information for fathers in all situations, including divorce.

National Fathers Resource Center
www.fathers4kids.com
Father's rights organization located in Dallas. Site includes resources to assist fathers who cannot come to their centers.

 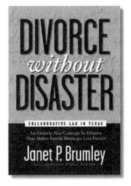